THE GLENS OF SILENCE

LANDSCAPES OF THE HIGHLAND CLEARANCES

DAVID CRAIG

DAVID PATERSON

The Glens of Silence

Where have I heard a silence before
Like this that only a lone bird's cries
And the sound of a brawling burn today
Serve in this wide empty glen but to emphasize?

Every doctor knows it—the stillness of foetal death…

Here is an identical silence, picked out
By a bickering burn and a lone bird's wheeple
—The foetal death in this great 'cleared' glen
Where the fear-thollaidh nan tighem* has done his foul work
—The tragedy of an unevolved people.

Hugh MacDiarmid

* Destroyer of homes

THE GLENS OF SILENCE

LANDSCAPES OF THE HIGHLAND CLEARANCES

TEXT BY DAVID CRAIG

PHOTOGRAPHS BY DAVID PATERSON

First published in Britain by
Birlinn Ltd., West Newington House,
10 Newington Road, Edinburgh EH9 1QS
and by
Wildcountry Press, Dochart House,
Killin, Perthshire FK21 8TN.

Jacket photograph: *Bourblaig, Ardnamurchan*
Title page: *Badbea, Caithness*

ISBN: 1 84158 325 1

British Library cataloguing applied for.

Craig, David
Paterson, David
The Glens of Silence
1. Scotland
2. History
3. Photography
4. Travel

Designed and produced by Wildcountry Press,
with thanks to Jim and Tom.
Originated and printed in China by Toppan.

House at Lonbain, Applecross, with the hills of Skye behind

CONTENTS

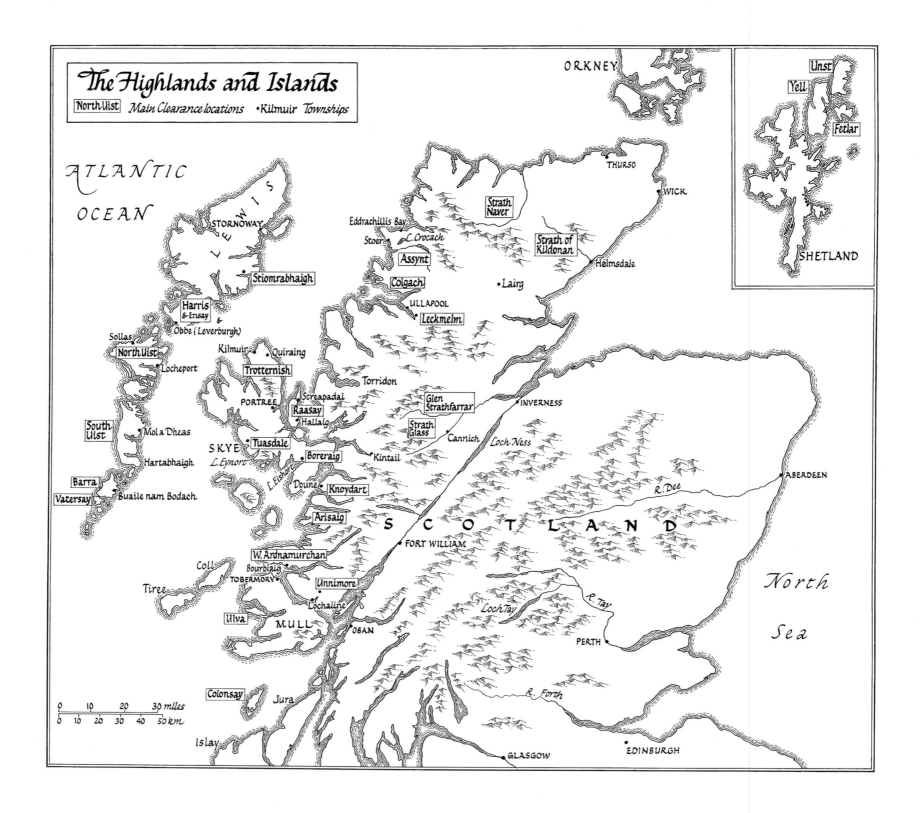

The Highlands and Islands

North Uist Main Clearance locations •Kilmuir Townships

ORKNEY
Unst
Yell
Fetlar
SHETLAND

ATLANTIC OCEAN

THURSO
WICK

LEWIS
STORNOWAY

Strath Naver
Eddrachillis Bay
Stoer L. Crocach
Assynt
Coigach
Strath of Kildonan
Helmsdale
Lairg

Stiomrabhaigh
ULLAPOOL
Leckmelm

Harris & Ensay
Obbe (Leverburgh)

Sollas
North Uist
Locheport

Kilmuir Quiraing
Trotternish
Torridon
Glen Strathfarrar
INVERNESS
Screapadal
PORTREE
Raasay
Hallaig
Strath Glass
Cannich Loch Ness

South Uist
Mol a Dheas
SKYE
Tuasdale
Boreraig
Kintail
L. Eynort
L. Eishort
Doune
Knoydart

Hartabhaigh

Barra
Vatersay Buaile nam Bodach
Arisaig

R. Dee
ABERDEEN

SCOTLAND

W. Ardnamurchan
Bourblaig
TOBERMORY
Unnimore
Lochaline

Coll
Tiree

FORT WILLIAM

North Sea

R. Tay
Loch Tay

Ulva
MULL
OBAN

PERTH

Colonsay
Jura

R. Forth

0 10 20 30 miles
0 10 20 30 40 50 km

Islay

GLASGOW
EDINBURGH

6

FOREWORD

That crustiest of conservatives, Dr Samuel Johnson, was once asked for his opinion of a newly-minted philosophical theory to the effect that the world around us exists only in our minds. Johnson, who was out walking at the time, took aim at a conveniently-placed, and very substantial-looking, stone. Kicking the stone hard and no doubt wincing as he did so, Johnson commented: "I refute it thus."

Samuel Johnson, as it happens, was one of the first to forecast, as early as the 1770s, the nature of the catastrophe that was about to engulf the Scottish Highlands and Islands as clanship collapsed and the region's former clan chiefs, in their new role as landed proprietors, began to treat people who had been their loyal followers as so many disposable obstacles in the way of their money-making plans. 'Their chiefs,' Johnson wrote of the north of Scotland's clansfolk, 'have already lost much of their influence, and as they degenerate from patriarchal rulers to rapacious landlords, they will divest themselves of the little that remains.'

Before delivering this gloomy but accurate prognosis as to Highlands and Islands prospects, Samuel Johnson—typically—travelled to the area and talked with its inhabitants. Now David Craig and David Paterson have done something similar, with a view to conveying the sheer scale of the calamity which Johnson's 'rapacious landlords' visited on their estates and on their tenantries, in the course of a desperate quest for the revenues needed to sustain the new and fashionably lavish lifestyles these same landlords had universally adopted.

The revenues in question were produced by turning over the bulk of the Highlands and Islands to incoming sheep farmers who paid far higher rents than those which could be got from the families who had previously occupied the

The cleared township of Suishnish in southern Skye, looking towards Rum which was itself entirely cleared of its people

land. Before this could happen and the farmers thus acquire the land, tenant after tenant, of course, had to be evicted. The ensuing removals and dispossessions—which often involved the obliteration of entire communities—became known as the Highland Clearances.

Today it is fashionable in some quarters to minimise the clearances; to say that their impact has been exaggerated; even to assert that they did not occur at all. In a pragmatic fashion of which Samuel Johnson would have approved, David Craig and David Paterson have demolished all such contentions. From Shetland to the Hebrides and from the Highland mainland's east coast to its west, they have demonstrated the actuality and the extent of clearance by photographing and describing the many places emptied by men who said, as the perpetrators of atrocities usually do, that they were acting in the cause of human progress. In the event, such progress as resulted from the Highland Clearances—and there was little of that—was achieved on the back of awful suffering. In David Paterson's fine photographs of where the evicted Highlanders lived and in David Craig's powerful evocations of how they responded to what was done to them, the victims of that suffering have an appropriate memorial.

James Hunter

INTRODUCTION

People streamed away from the Highlands and Islands of Scotland from the late 18th century onwards, for at least six generations. Many thousands went more or less voluntarily, driven by lack of land, forever-rising rents, compulsory services to their landlords, and the hardship of living through bad years when hay and corn were mildewed by wet summers. Many thousands were forced out by writs for arrears of rent or at the order of an estate whose managers wanted to create a sheep-ranch out of the many smallholdings or crofts and so treble or quadruple the rental income.

Those parts of Scotland had become vulnerable to drastic change. In the aftermath of the Jacobite Rising (1745-6) the landed gentry could no longer act as clan chieftains. Their feudal jurisdictions, the carrying of weapons, and the wearing of traditional dress were now forbidden. More fundamentally, the rich men and their ladies began to look to Edinburgh and London as the places to be—to network with the Lowland ruling class, take houses for 'the season' or permanently, and go to grand parties. This was expensive. The low rentals paid by their poor or middling tenants could not fund a metropolitan way of life. The old estates must be made to pay via the growing market for wool, mutton and later, kelp. There was no longer room for the families who made a bare living and fed and clothed themselves with their own produce. At best they could provide labour for enlarged farms and new-built mansions. At worst they could be exported to the 'virgin' lands of America and Australia. If they would not accept a passage on aship, they would have to be removed under duress.

It is these evictions that are called the Clearances, still a by-word, as when an islander says about the closure of a village school: 'It's as bad as the Clearances'. The estate men might burn the roof of a cottage to make it uninhabitable and prevent re-occupation. Or they might nail the door shut. Or they might tear off the turf upper section of the walls and re-use the stones to make a sheep-fank or a dyke. In extreme cases—more and more common by the 1850s—they might destroy the family's store of fresh milk and butter, cream and cheese, or throw out and smash the family's gear and crockery, or injure the people, often the women, with clubs as they tried to fight against the evictions.

Many emigrating Highlanders settled well in the new country, Canada or New Zealand, where land was abundant and more or less free. So a Benbecula man writes home from Manitoba in 1883: 'We have got plenty of land, very good water, any amount of timber; also we are not under bondage to any man, as we have been in Benbecula. I have also to tell you that I sowed twelve bushels of potatoes, four bushels of barley, half a bushel of white beans, carrots, onions and turnips, and to look after them coming up is a glory you would not believe, and we are thinking ourselves happy that we left Benbecula in time.'[1] Many other emigrants struggled desperately to establish themselves in the forests of the New World—if they had survived the vile conditions on board ship. A postman on Skye told me how his two great-uncles were evicted twice in ten years and took the boat across the Atlantic: 'Their wives landed in North America, both widowed and each with babes in arms born on the voyage.' In one year's emigration from Scotland and Ireland, out of 106,000 people 17,200 died on the voyage or within a few months of landing.[2]

Smallholders—crofters, subsistence farmers, peasants—are invariably harrowed by harsh conditions and rough-and-ready or downright brutal management, in whatever country they live. The parallels with Scotland are worldwide. Forty years ago in Sri Lanka I learned from the new generation of Ceylonese historians how cultivators in the Kandy area were dispossessed by British settlers. The village lands were seized and planted with coffee trees. Paths to the wells were closed by fences. When the Kandyans broke the fences and tore up the trees, they were given a month in prison for damaging fences and a year plus fifty lashes for barking or uprooting trees. You were also liable to be dispossessed of your land unless you could prove with title-deeds that you owned it, which was impossible because most deeds were on strips of palm leaf and had turned to dust long before. So the incomers seized the prime land, just as the Highland hill pastures were taken from the crofting townships and let out to graziers from the Lowlands and the north of England. The Ceylon expropriations were happening in the 1840s. At that time, as the Potato Famine made life impossible in the Highlands, mass clearance set in on Skye, Raasay, Barra, the Uists and elsewhere. A few years later the most striking of all the clearance parallels occurred on the north island of New Zealand, in the Parihaka area between the beautiful symmetrical mountain of Taranaki (Mount Egmont) and the western coast. Three million acres were taken from the Maori by force of arms and sold off to settlers. Villages were emptied and the cottage timbers smashed. Detail after detail exactly replicated what had happened in Scotland. Potato crops were destroyed. Starving people were put to road work on a minimum wage so as to 'carefully avoid all pampering'. The ownership of dogs was taxed or prohibited. The similarities are endless—there was even a stream which was given the name of Waitotora, 'water of long blood', to commemorate a pitched battle against eviction, just as there is a burn in North Uist called Abhainn na Fala, 'river of blood', after the Sollas women's fight with constables and estate men in 1849.

The Parihaka people mounted a campaign of nonviolent resistance and their saintly heroism led eventually, after much hardship and the imprisonment of leaders, to victory of a sort.[3] There is still a Maori community there—now struggling against industrial pollution of their fishing grounds—just as there are still communities at Achiltibuie in Coigach, at Cliad in Barra and at Kilmuir in Skye. Most Highland townships surrendered, and the Crofters' War to reclaim them did not happen until the 1880s. The glens were emptied, and nowadays there is only a thin scattering of cottages in Strath Oykel and Strath Naver, in Fetlar and North Yell, in Knoydart and West Ardnamurchan, in Raasay and Minginish. People were bound to make for the towns and overseas, as virgin lands and the cash economy beckoned. The pity of it is that the wrench of parting from your native place was made all the more cruel by so much callous illtreatment. So it goes, the world over. What is special about the Highland Clearances is that they happened in a part of our country which we now see to be supremely handsome, with its giant contours and sublime interweaving of the sea and the land, still peopled by men and women who know what happened to their grandparents or greatgrandparents—who understand the hard graft and skill with which they won their livelihoods—and the ordeal of dispossession inflicted on them by their economic masters.

The Clearances have been chronicled and analysed by John Prebble and James Hunter, Eric Richards and J. M. Bumsted. What these historians have made little use of is the memoirs of the people themselves, passed down usually by word of mouth and still current all over the Highlands. As Hunter himself says in *The Making of the Crofting Community* (1976; 2002), 'it is possible to reconstruct the events' but 'not the emotions' of the people from official records. Wherever possible we have listened to the crofters in finding out what happened in this glen or that island, whether it reaches us directly through the talk of the people we have met or through the testimony of the many hundreds of witnesses at government commissions in the later 19th century. And we have gone to the places where eviction happened, to look at the furrowed ground, at the stone walls, the lintels still in place, at the wells and ditches and other small traces which are the almost indelible features of a way of life.

Sometimes you warm to the goodness of a basin or trough of old arable land protected by rising ground against the ocean and its salt-gust. Sometimes you marvel that so many people could have subsisted on land so shelterless. A hundred years ago a boatman from Rona, north of Raasay, east of Skye, recalled how evicted people went 'to the churchyard in their grief at being separated from their homes' and took 'handfuls of the soil and grass that covered the graves of their kindred, as mementoes'.

It is not surprising, when you feel the green pastures of Vatersay beneath your feet or walk beside the clear brown waters of the River Glass in Inverness-shire, that the Highlands and Islands engendered so deep an attachment.

David Craig

SHETLAND

The strand at Burrafirth, Unst

House and shed at Gutcher, Yell

Unst and Yell in north Shetland are remarkably similar, both naturally and humanly. Unst's northern end is split by the deep inlet of Burra Firth, Yell's by Gloup Voe. On each island the western arm, once closely crofted, has been emptied by clearance. On Unst the cleft carries on, after a short land bridge, into Loch of Cliff, a narrow water two-and-a-half miles long. Here the settlement history has been reversed. Cliff on the east side, being easy to reach and convenient for enlarged farming, was emptied by the factor in the mid 19th century. On the west side, remote and steeply sloping Petester was owned by a different estate and lived on until the 1960s.

Petester, which probably means Picts' pasture, is unique in the terracing of its townland, which is as elaborate as a thousand hill-villages in Greece, say, or Nepal. The ground folds steeply into the burn. Especially on the north slope, the lush turf is belted and squared into a whole mesh of little fields. This inby land must have been as hard to break in and then to work as any in the British Isles. People nearby, in Queyhouse and Baltasound, still speak with grim admiration about the toil it cost the Petester people to till that ground, with spades, and creels on backs, and sledges dragged by horses. It is a green network now, grazed only by sheep, with no catch of oats and potatoes held in its loops.

The contrast with Cliff on the opposite shore is poignant. Here the land is wide and comfortable. Access to the harbours and fisher-towns of Haraldswick and Balta a few miles east will have been easy. So the laird and the factor turned it into a sheep-farm and got rid of the people, for example a family called Johnson. They came home, according to Mrs Sutherland who lives at the head of Burra Firth, 'and found their roof gone and the old folk sitting on the ground amongst their gear'. An old woman who was refusing to leave was sent some miles away on an errand 'and when she got back her house had been pulled down and its stones built up into a dyke'.

The regime in Unst and North Yell was in the hands of Major Cameron and his farmer-agent John Walker. According to Andrew Spence, a crofter from Brecken a mile and a half north-east of Cliff, 'Walker wronged every person, and would not have cared whether the sheep were put under a dyke or what we did with them'.[1] According to William Tulloch, the shopkeeper and postmaster at Cullivoe in north-east Yell, Walker 'was hated by the North Yell people as much as the Evil One himself'.[2] The means of eviction were straightforward. He doubled rents. When the oats and barley were blasted by hail early in the winter of 1869 and the same storms made both herring and white fishing almost impossible, the crofter families fell into arrears and could be warned out. In any case their leases were for ten years and the tenants could then be thrown out 'without legal warning' or else were obliged to 'double the previous year's rent for every year'. Money apart, the conditions of tenancy were like fetters. Wendy Gear of Gutcher, all of whose grandparents were evicted by Walker, has found from the North Yell valuation rolls that 'No tenant is allowed any privilege outside the boundaries of his farm', or to have access to peat, seaweed, or sand, or to keep a dog, or to sell straw, turnips, hay, or dung.[3] So the means of life were denied to the people. And so it was across the crofting counties from Barra to East Sutherland.

The most crippling embargo was on the use of the hill-grazing or scattald. According to Andrew Spence, when Walker became factor he 'laid on a sum of £1 on the rent for the hill, and after that he railed in the hill and took it away altogether'.[4] The rail was a well-built stone dyke six feet high – quite as formidable as the long walls on Fetlar or the epic wall built on Rousay in Orkney for General Traill when he cleared the whole west end of the island.[5] On Unst you can see Walker's wall running north and south on the 100-ft contour east of Cliff in a remorselessly efficient remake of the much older dyke built out of big single stones a few feet down the hill.

The rancour and hardship of the clearance on Unst and Yell are still remembered. Walker was burnt in effigy. He had lived up to his role as the

Evil One by going round at night digging up sheeps' heads from middens to check whether the earmarks belonged to the croft or to one of his new farms. The parents of Grace Mann, who could still tell me her story at Mid Yell in 1989, were evicted from Walker farmland above Basta Voe, from a place 'that had plenty of sheep and grew good crops'. When her people had to leave their home, according to Mrs Odie who runs the Burravoe Museum, 'They came away by boat, and to keep the baby warm they heated beach stones and wrapped them in a cloth.'

On these islands the history is personal and near. John Henderson of Gloup lives near a noble sculpture of a woman with a baby in her arms. It commemorates the storm of July 1881 which sank six of the lightweight fishing boats called sixerns and drowned thirty-six men. He rowed us across the voe to West a Firth, from which his grandfather was evicted. Sixteen tenants lived there in 1867; two and a pauper by 1871; just the one shepherd in 1884. Shells of houses are spread widely over ample fields. John could name them all, including The Neap, the home of his father's mother, who died when John was eleven. He did not idealise his forebears. 'They were wild!' he said with some relish. 'They were aalways pinchin sheep.' He also knew the value of life in such a place. 'When the sun is oot,' he said as he rowed us back with the wind behind him, 'and the voe is calm, you can see the flukes on the bottom. We ran aal aboot the geos and the cliffs. We didna hae much. But we could *see*'—he paused to find the words—'we could see the *nature* of the *world*, really.'

House and steading at Cliff, Unst

Loch of Cliff, Unst

Abandoned croft-house at Quoys, Unst

Boat at Brough jetty, Fetlar

FETLAR – SHETLAND

Much of Fetlar, the most easterly island in Shetland, was bought in 1815 by Sir Arthur Nicolson. He was a man with big ideas, who believed he was descended from Arthur, the mythical king. His biggest idea was the clearance of Fetlar, carried out between 1822 and 1856. He made his tenants build walls to partition off the land occupied by clusters of crofts. Then he evicted most of the people from inside each wall and replaced them with shepherds. In the near destitution after the Potato Famine of 1846–7, the families were given handouts of meal on condition that they did some walling.[1] The drystone dykes still crawl in all directions like grey chains clasped round the hips and shoulders of the island.

At first Nicolson had threatened to evict anybody who worked at the Atlantic whaling because they were earning cash outside the system which forced most people to fish inshore and trade their catch for goods at the laird's price in the laird's shops. The men marched to Nicolson's new Gothic mansion in 1820 to protest against this crippling bind.[2] In a few years 'the laird's mark was on the doors'–a chalked cross signifying eviction. Gruting in the north-east had twelve inhabited houses in 1821–only one forty years later. Urie in the north-west shrank from twelve houses to two. The families were forbidden to remove fixtures from their houses (cupboards, box-beds) and one man was fined £3 for taking his barn roof with

him when he relocated to Unst.[3] Both places are empty now, their eternal green blotted white with sheep. In Gruting Nicolson commanded his masons to build a sort of ornamental stone tower with a wooden storey on top. The circular stub of it suggests a broch–another of Nicolson's harkings back to the age of warrior chieftains? Two ten-foot pillars of solid stone have fallen out of the porch and lie amongst nettles. Two more made in sections still stand, looking like something out of Highgate Cemetery. It's said that Nicolson slept in this staggering folly for only one night and was disturbed by ghosts. The place functioned for a time as an office where the crofters came with their rents–and to be told when they were being increased.[4] By a neat scam, when rents were raised the laird went on paying his rates on the basis of the smaller sum.[5]

Fulmars nest on the old tower now, and on the ground near the ill-made dyke that surrounds the place. The brooding bird sits tight and her or his mate flies at you with not a flap of its tapering wings, fixing its black eye on you as it whisks just overhead. In the lush valley nearby called Vats of Evey a few cattle graze among the many lines of turf dyke marking old field edges. A little west, between Ness of Gruting and Swart Houll, stone after stone declares the long habitation of the place. A girdle of boulders set on edge like shields stretches from the Tarri Geos at the cliff to the

ruined croft at Muckligarth—probably a pickie dyke, a settlement boundary marked out by the Picts who had the island before the Norsemen came. Across the Wick of Ness between Gruting and the final northward-pointing headland you can see the gaunt two-storey shell of Smithfield House. It was built in 1815 for Gilbert Smith, Nicolson's factor. His father was known to be a press-gang informer during the Napoleonic Wars.[6] When Smithfield House was built, a woman called Merran Jamieson let down her hair and cursed the place: 'Da's left me destitute. But a'll repay dee. Dy fine hoose'll go into ruin, da birds o da air'll use it fir dir restin place an dey'll be sun, mon an stars tro da waas. Da baests o da field'll mak it into a dunghill an every root branch o de will vanish fae da face o da ert, dy name die oot laek a withered leaf!'

Such curses are the hot, helpless breath of the oppressed, the heart of a heartless situation. Even the sober language of the legal documents has a deadly gravity. The summons of eviction served by Nicolson's lawyers on William Johnson, tenant of Aithbank, on 28 March 1842 goes in part: '[Johnson] ought and SHOULD be DECERNED and ORDAINED to flit and remove himself, his Family, Servants, Cottars, and Dependants, Goods and Gear, forth and from his said Possession, and to leave the same void and redd, at the turn of Martinmas next, in this present year, to the effect that the Complainer, or others in his name, may then enter thereto, and peaceably possess and enjoy the same in all time coming...' The plain and helpless language of the underdog survives in a letter written by John Thomson from London on 23 July 1852 as he was about to embark as a deckhand on a windjammer bound for Sydney: 'I here [sic] that there is a great overturns in Fetlar, with the tennents and Sir Arthur, and my father [probably Alex Thomason of Uskister—now a ruin two miles east of Nicolson's derelict mansion] is among the rest I suppose but I can do nothing in it and so the poor man must do the best he can at present.'

Uskister is one of seventeen clusters of homesteads that occupied the western end of the island. If you leave the road from Brough Lodge to the Oddsta ferry pier at the cattle-grid, then follow the long wall north-east, you come to Urie. In its day it was a full-fledged settlement. The biggest ruin is the fine haa built for a laird who came to Fetlar from Perthshire in 1707. The detail of the masonry is very fine. The rebates of the window jambs are whole stones chiselled into shape to take the frames. More graved stones lie amongst rubble nearby. A low stone roof in the ground beside the burn is shown to have been a watermill by a section of grindstone lying beside it, and the burn a little uphill has clearly been dammed and ditched to run water through the mill. There

was a small shop here in Nicolson's time. The local name for a cottage to the north is the Gudeman's House—home of a priest before the Reformation. To the north again, on the shore of Urie Ness, two dykes angling towards each other in shallow water are the remains of a harbour. Nicolson lived in the fine house until he decided it was below his dignity and commissioned his misshapen mansion at Ness of Brough.[7]

There is an odd quirk in the two kilometres of wall between the road and the sea. It curves out and back again in a little bracket six metres long. Was it to make one side of a shelter for the wallers as they fettled their way across the miles of bents and heather? Or was it a gesture to defy the pitiless straight rule of the landlord, a sort of crofters' folly to answer the laird's towers? Walls were so crucial to Fetlar that they bred their own

myths. One of the longest runs south-west from the shore at Muckle Funziegord Geo and ends up nowhere on the south-west flank of the island's highest upland, Vord Hill. It is said that the nearest farmer, at Colbinstoft, was 'troubled by the inroads of his neighbours' cattle, and vowed one night that he would give one of his best oxen if there was a wall built there in the morning. When he got up the wall was there, and his best ox lay dead in the byre.'[8]

So the stones of Fetlar remain, the fine articulation of houses, fields, and kailyards dismembered and simplified, while the builders and their descendants have mostly gone—with mixed feelings. Eileen Hughson of Houbie told me that her mother, whose people had been cleared from Colbinstoft, 'always said it was a good thing, to get out of poverty and go to New Zealand'. Robert Johnson, the crofter historian from Mid Yell across the water, summed up the outcome when he wrote that 'in thirty years (1831–61) three hundred people —mostly the young active men and women—had had to find homes outwith the island.'[9] Today the place has become a kind of haven for English people with particular ideals—an astronomer at Tresta who has brought a powerful telescope from Edinburgh to view the clearest stars in the British Isles, an archivist at Houbie who is collecting the poignant evidence of how Fetlar endured the Clearance and its aftermath.

Houses and field-walls at Urie, Fetlar

The 'Observatory' at Brough Lodge

SUTHERLAND

Loch Crocach with Suilven, Cul Mor, Cul Beg & Stac Pollaidh, Assynt

Strath Naver Parish Church, Syre

STRATH NAVER – SUTHERLAND

S trath Naver is not one of those cleared areas where the settlements were on small pockets of arable ground–the alluvial fans of eastern South Uist, for example, or the north shore of Loch Seilg in Lewis, or the western end of Ardna-murchan. The valley is majestically long with a level floor on which good harvests of barley, hay and turnips can still be cropped. Famines or very lean years occurred from time to time, and were used by the estate managers as grounds for declar-ing the place fit only for sheep. Three or four gen-erations before the clearances, Daniel Defoe noted on his tour of Great Britain that the strath was an exporter of horses, especially to Orkney.[1]

In 1884 Angus Mackay, who remembered the evic-tions in detail, testified to the Napier Commis-sioners, who were sailing round the Highlands and Islands inquiring into 'the Condition of the Crofters and Cottars', that 'The people had plenty of flocks of goats, sheep, horses, and cattle, and they were living happy. . .with flesh and fish and butter and cheese and fowl and potatoes and kail and milk too. There was no want of anything with them; and they had the Gospel preached to them at both ends of the strath.'[2]

The waters run for twenty-seven miles from the head of Loch Naver to where the river enters the Pentland Firth below an extraordinary headland patrolled by mewing buzzards and overwhelmed by sandblow to a height of three hundred feet. Here is Bettyhill, where Angus Mackay met the Commissioners. It was named after the Countess of Sutherland, who with her husband owned the largest landholding in the United Kingdom. Her managers, most notably William Young, Patrick Sellar, and Francis Suther, dumped the cleared folk between an upland like the Gobi Desert, the most dangerous sea channel in the British Isles, and hummocky ground so rocky that, as Robert Mackay from the highest croft remarked to me, 'You'd have to blast to make a basement'.

The evictions swept the whole strath bare from its source to near its mouth, during and after the Napoleonic Wars. In 1819, the year of the second and final bout, 1,228 people were evicted and their roofs burnt. They included the family of William Campbell, a kiltmaker, who lived along-side fifteen other families at Grummore, on the north shore of the loch below the slopes of Meall a' Bhrollaich. His daughter Minnie told her story around 1910 to her great-grandson's wife, Daisy MacEwen, and she passed it on to me. 'They went down the strath to the sea and walked all along the shore—well, near the shore. What a walk—carrying wee bairns. And they had cattle with them to start with. But when they got to Dunnet Head [more than fifty miles from their old home], the natives, the Caithnessians, pinched their cattle during the night. . .And they made a divot house, in Mey, and they tried to break in a bit of the heather.'

This must have been one of those epic treks, through crushing hardships and into unknown country and a foreign language, which the peo-ples of the world have been forced to endure time and time again: the cleared people of Strath Kildonan, not far from Strath Naver, who fled southward from Hudson Bay and the frosts of North Dakota to Ontario, a thousand miles from where the emigrant ship had left them; the Navajo in 1863, forced to abandon their fields and peach orchards in Canyon de Chelley and march to a concentration camp at Fort Sumner; the Armenians in 1915, fleeing their massacred villages and trekking southward into Syria, har-ried by police and bandits...

The aftermath of the exodus could be cruel in subtler ways. According to Daisy McEwen's daughter Margaret Hughes, Minnie Campbell remembered 'how her mother was "never right" after the eviction. . .not because of the physical hardships and shock involved, but because her two sons, Minnie's brothers, had been enlisted in the Countess of Sutherland's regiment to fight in the Peninsular War, and their mother was still waiting confidently for their return. . .Somehow she felt that the enforced move, with no means of leaving a message for them, meant that they were indeed dead, at least in that she could never hope to see them again.'

This is the most distressing personal crux in the gamut of the evictions. Here is the intimate history of the Clearances. How many thousands of parents and other relatives were made distraught by severance from their loved ones? To return safely from those foreign wars was an epic in itself. When the 78th Highland Regiment was paid off in Madras, 'ten thousand sea-miles from their cool blue Highlands', they had to make their own way home. Their anguished determination to get back was put into lyrical words by the soldier poet Christopher Macrae of Kintail:

[We were] told everywhere
that there was no ship, no boat nor sail.
It is a pity that I am not as light
as the hawk, slim-flying in the sky.
I would take the desert road
and I would not rest in the tree-tops.
In spite of the violence of Turkey
I would pass it like a lark in the sun.
And I would make a complaint in London
that would bring us all home.[3]

These were men who might well have been conscripted under the Act of 1797 which commandeered an unmarried son from each family, or, cruellest of all, they might have been pressed to enlist by an offer from the landlord which they could not refuse. If a crofter's son would not enlist in the Countess's regiment, the 93rd, the family could be evicted because, she wrote, they 'need no longer be considered a credit to Sutherland, or any advantage over sheep or any useful animal'.[4] Or again—according to a letter of about 1807 shown me by Frances MacDonald at her house beside the salmon falls of the river Shin near Lairg—the factor would offer a crofter a piece of land in exchange for his son's enlisting, then renege on the promise 'to his very great Loss and eminent Ruin'.

When the Sutherlands had finished turning their vast estate into sheep ranches, Strath Naver was left as it is today, like the other glens of the far north, Halladale, Kildonan, Fleet, Brora, Loth: an artery of fertility in the body of the moors, as well-watered and habitable as any dale in Yorkshire or Cumbria, with not a village to speak of, where almost the only people to be seen are passing through or visiting briefly as guests of a millionaire owner to stalk stags or kill salmon.

Grummore township, with Loch Naver and Ben Klibreck

Ruin at Grumbeg, Strath Naver

Fields near Achargary, Strath Naver

The sheep-fank at Costly, Kildonan

STRATH OF KILDONAN – SUTHERLAND

The sinuous long strath of Kildonan in easter Sutherland runs south-east from Badanloch, marooned on an ocean of moorland, down the River Helmsdale to the town of that name–a neat settlement with grid-plan streets, contrived by the Sutherland estate in the early 19th century to accustom the cleared people from the interior to a new life as fisherfolk. The floodplain of the river is green with goodness for animals and people, sheltered comfortably between 2,000-ft mountains with gradual contours. With all that it's silent. To be in it is like having a membrane drawn tightly over our ears, blanking out what we should be hearing: hens clucking, cows lowing, dogs barking, the shouts and busy noises of people. We should be seeing the sources of the sounds, tractors and children and farm animals, we should be seeing washing blowing on lines, and gardens brimming with vegetables and flowers round each cluster of cottages.

Nowadays in Kildonan we hear little but the grating of sheep, the bellowing of red-deer stags in October, the exhausts of the keeper's or sheep-farmer's Land Rover, and perhaps the crack of a rifle as a visitor from one of the lodges bags a stag and gets something to show for his £1,500 a week. The strath has been empty of normal life since much of it was cleared in 1813–4 under the supervision of Patrick Sellar, a well-off farmer from Moray across the water, and the rest in 1818–21 under the supervision of Francis Suther, a farm manager from one of the English estates of the Duke of Stafford, the Countess of Sutherland's husband.

A glimpse of the earlier Clearance has come down by word of mouth. Betty Fraser is the earliest cleared person whose photograph I have come across.[1] She was born in 1804 and died in 1907. Her great-grandsons Alec and Jock Cuthbert of Gartymore told me that she would 'hardly talk to anybody at all about the. . .evictions'. The nub of her story was this: 'They had no shoes in those days, of course, they always went just barefoot, and when Betty was coming over the mountain there, over Eldrable, she was with her wee sister, and they each had a sheep with them–they were like a pet, I suppose. And the shepherd who kept the farm for the estate down there at Port Gower, when he saw them he set his dogs on the sheep and worried them.'

The estate had been bought by Stafford with money made from canals and coal-mines in the English Midlands. He aimed to make his property pay by turning it into large sheep-farms with tenants, especially from the north of England. The people living along the fertile bottomlands of the glens, to the north in Halladale and Naver, to the west in Brora and Fleet, were in no condition to resist the swingeing scythe of clearance. They had been demoralised by hunger in the wet years of 1812 and 1817 when potatoes were spoiled and meal was scarce. Many of the relocated people had to sleep on the shore, eat cockles and mussels, and pawn their bedding to fishermen. Their old homelands are still remembered: by a veteran farmer in Western Ontario who knows his forebears came from Brora without being too sure of its whereabouts; by a woman near Dornoch who knows that a forebear six generations ago 'saw a red glow' in the sky as the estate men burned the roofs of the houses at Lettaidh in Strath Fleet. The foundation stones lie low in the good grass of the place, while across the valley in Inchcape houses still stand and are lived in, because there a man called Sutherland pulled the factor off his horse when he came with his summonses to quit, during the Napoleonic Wars.

The Kildonan people found it hard to make a living in the new town of Helmsdale. When they tried to fish, they found that many of the best grounds were monopolised by boats from the ports on the other shore of the Moray Firth, from Findhorn to Rosehearty. Gathering shellfish from the rich mussel-beds to eke out their food was treated as poaching, because the mussels were reserved for bait.[2] Two generations after the Clearances the Kildonaners were represented before the Napier Commissioners by Angus Sutherland, a crofter's son who taught in Glasgow. His testimony is one of the most closely-argued in all the 46,750 questions put by the Commission. His gist was that 1,574 people were removed from the 130,000 acres of arable and hill grazing which they occupied and 'compressed into about 3,000 acres of the most barren and sterile land in the parish'. They received no compensation for 'the land which had been reclaimed and put under crop by the crofters prior to the clearance. This can be conclusively proved from the amount of green with the plough ridges still distinguishable.'[3]

Such a place was, and is, Costly. This is the clachan from which Betty Fraser was evicted. In the usual way it has somehow disappeared from present-day maps. Not even a name is there. We only found it with the help of a sketch-map drawn by Jock Cuthbert in his house in Gartymore. It lies on the true left bank of the river, where the Allt Breac runs down out of the hills. The green land there has the tender goodness of ground anciently tilled. Most of the house-stones were built up again into circular fanks, often by the cleared people themselves, to accommodate the sheep who had replaced them. The salmon and deer which had added wild meat to their diet were now the exclusive property of the owners and their guests.

In the resettlement areas where the people were dumped—West Helmsdale, Port Gower and Marrel for example—they were 'so huddled together that a man cannot walk round his own house without trespassing on his neighbour's land.

Poultry cannot be kept, for if they stray half-a-dozen yards they are into a neighbour's corn.'[4] Much of this terrain should never have been lived in and it punishes people to this day. Betty Fraser's great-grandson Alec, for example, had difficulty using his crutches because the ground outside his house was so steep.

In his evidence to the Commissioners Angus Sutherland played down the famines of his grandfather's generation, and this is typical. You almost never hear a word of the old starvations when Highlanders speak about the past, presumably because lean years were such irresistible acts of God that they did not engender stories of grievance and injustice. What people felt was that they

had lost their old independent footing in the world. They looked for it in Canada. Many Gunns and Sutherlands ended up in the graveyard of West Gwillimbury in Ontario—Alexander Gunn for example, who died on 23 March 1839, and whose marble headstone identifies him as 'A Native of the Parish of Kildonan'. He and his people had survived perhaps the most gruelling journey in our history. For years they had voyaged and walked, from Wick via Stromness in Orkney to the River of Strangers, which flows into Hudson Bay just north of Churchill. From there they struggled through blizzards and plagues of grasshoppers to the Red River, in what is now Manitoba, and on to the Dakotah plains where the Ojibwa and Dakota people employed them as 'hewers of wood and drawers of water' and taught them to hunt buffalo.[5]

The furthest north trace of a Kildonaner is the lower half of a rough-cut gravestone which lies amongst grey shingle, scrub willow, and bearberry on the shore of the estuary at Churchill. The upper half, now lost, used to say 'John', according to Florence Beardy, a woman of Highland/Cree descent who took me to the spot. The lower half still bears, in chiselled cursive lettering, the name Sutherland and the date 1813.

Outline of a house at Lettaidh, Strath Fleet, east Sutherland

The Strath of Kildonan at Duible, with Beinn Dubhainn

The last house in Glen Loth, east Sutherland

Hilltop sheep-fank in Strath Brora

Sunset on Loch Assynt

ASSYNT – SUTHERLAND

In West Sutherland the mountains stand about like great blue-grey animals asleep on their feet. In the moorland spaces between them, on the banks of burns and rivers and the shores of lochs like plaques of black glass, you can find settlements abandoned two hundred years ago, if you look hard enough.

Bad a' Ghrianan beside Loch Crocach, five miles inland from Achmelvich; Dubh Chlais and Druim Suardalain, between Glen Canisp Lodge and the River Inver; Ach na h' Eaglais overlooking Loch Assynt, two miles north of Inchnadamph; Glenleraig in the jungly dale between Loch an Leothaid and the south shore of Eddrachillis Bay: all these little places were cleared in the second decade of the 19th century.

What was in it for the people was relief from the mildew which blighted the hay and corn of the inland smallholdings. What was in it for the estate, the Sutherlands' huge spread now being factored by Francis Suther in the aftermath of Patrick Sellar, were the trebled rentals which flowed from the fusing of many little townships into one big sheepwalk. A chief among the new tenants was the Sutherland's under-manager, an ex-Army man called Gunn, the Chief-apparent of his clan.

On most days in the tourist season a large gaggle of cars are parked near the mournful wreckage of Ardvreck Castle on Loch Assynt. A crumbling tower, the story of a Cavalier (the Duke of Montrose) on his way to execution–this is what is wanted by the calendar photographers and the tourists of all nations with their cameras. If you look up the grassy bluff east of the road at the right moment, you can see the gables of an equally significant ruin, showing like a pair of deer's ears turned to stone. This is the shell of the biggest house in Ach na h' Eaglais (or Kirkton), cleared in 1819 to make a sheep farm for one Charles Clarke. Hereabouts 135 people lived in 27 households: MacLeods and MacDonalds, MacRaes, MacKenzies and MacIvers.[1] This main house is twenty feet from ground to ridge, surely built for the farmer just after the evictions. (He went bankrupt six years later.)

The usual roomy post-Clearance field with an ill-made, rickety dyke round it lies nearby. How many family homes were dismantled to make this walling? Five other shells and little walled enclosures show in the grass nearby–lush grass, 'the richest pasture imaginable' in Gunn's words.[2] The land here is a resurgence of the limestone which runs northward in a colossal reef to plunge and resurface at Durness. This natural fertiliser makes the whole place juicy-green summer and winter. On a further ridge east of the clachan an unexpected elm grows straight out from the crag, then upwards in a flourish of leaves. If the guillotine of clearance had not fallen, the children and grandchildren of MacIvers and MacRaes would have been climbing out along it to sit or swing; the more daring would have been clambering up the little cliff. The people, unfortunately, were 'a useless body', 'idle and slovenly', 'more indolent than any of their neighbours and more unprincipled in their morals', according to under-manager Gunn.[3] Amazing how undeserving people are when you covet their land! So out they went.

Was it cruelly done? Or with meek compliance? It depends who you believe. Gunn says that 'they did not even utter a murmur' when they were evicted and 'assisted the Ground Officer when he was going through the ceremony of putting out their fires.'[4] On the other hand a labourer called William MacKenzie testified to Napier that Colin MacRae, a neighbour on the Eddrachillis shore where hundreds of Assynt families were resettled, 'remembers the extinguishing of his father's fire at Achnaheglish, when the victims went to cook a little food for their famished and frightened children, exposed to any inclemency and sheltered like fugitives.'[5] So either ex-Lieutenant Gunn was putting a smooth face on the eviction when he reported to his employers, or the crofter saw that mortal event, the dousing forever of the family fire, as a piece of real ill-treatment.

To the north, Bad a' Ghrianan, (drying-place or sunny spot) was for nine years (1812–21) a perch for families cleared from elsewhere in the interior and on their way out to the coast at Stoer or Achmelvich. It is reached via a narrow glen beyond Rhicarn on the road north from Lochinver. Wrinkles of turf-dyke footings and a much more extensive ring-dyke mark where people herded their animals and kept them grazing outside the arable ground. Long-horned, long-haired Highland cattle browse there now. A cottage has been re-roofed and re-pointed. A potato croft is full of food in the early autumn. A new forest has been deer-fenced. Civilisation is returning to these parts since the Assynt Crofters' Trust bought this part of Sutherland from Edmund Vestey, Master of the Queen's Horse and inheritor of a fortune made from frozen New Zealand mutton.

A mile further on Loch Crocach (antlered loch) comes brimming in from southward. Now the ruined village shows up. The biggest house has a complete north gable and a fireplace crowned by a massive, well-masoned lintel. Several house outlines can be made out on a ledge of well-drained, fertile ground. A small enclosure, possibly a kail-yard, lies between houses and loch. MacLeods, Kerrs and MacKaskles lived here for a while. Their absence presses on the eardrums and the brain. It's hard to leave this place. The liquid black metal of Loch Crocach, with its many bays and headlands, is punctured now and again by a rising trout. I listen and look. No black-throated diver

skreighs or makes its dark crucifix on the sky. The high-shouldered creatures, Suilven and Glas Bheinn and Quinag, stand up to east and south, layered in their weeping mists. I could walk on for miles. The path is a trod, grown over thickly now with heather and bracken, twisting away northwards. According to the householder down at Rhicarn, the people from Drumbeg on the Eddrachillis shore came this way to church at Lochinver—at least a three-hour walk. No doubt they included descendants of the 'idle' and 'unprincipled' people cleared out by Gunn in the 1820s.

The people from Ach na h' Eaglais were made to settle in places like Culkein Drumbeg on the

Eddrachillis shore and Rubha Stoer which bounds the bay in the west. William MacKenzie told Napier that 'when they found a resting place at all in their native land, it was on the poorest scraps, rocks, and bogs, and often put in amongst the poorest crofters, subdividing their lots, and intensifying their poverty'.[6] The sloping townland of Culkein is so stony that it's hard to tell a ruin from a heap of cleared field-stones or a heap from a natural outcrop. The headland at Stoer is treeless and shelterless, scathed by harsh Atlantic winds. Gunn had to admit that 'most of those who went to Rhue Store [sic] in pretty good circumstances are already [by December 1819] so poor as not to be able to purchase their share of a boat and the necessary fishing implements'.[7] We can hear their anguish at displacement in the almost biblical words of Murdoch Kerr, a fisherman from Achmelvich: 'Have they not been the destruction of the place to us? Have they not sent us down to the rocks, and the shore of the sea?'[8]

Bad a' Grianan, Loch Crocach, with the mountains of Assynt

House at Druim Suardalain, Glen Canisp

Lochan Fionnlaidh and Cul Mor, Assynt

Tholl fhasgnaidh, or winnowing door, at Druim Suardalain

Modern-day crofting at Elphin, west Sutherland

ROSS-SHIRE

Shieldaig (Herring Bay) and the Torridon hills

The Coigach hills from Drumrunie

Without the wholehearted fight by the people of Coigach against eviction in 1852–3, it seems unlikely that there would be a decent village in Achiltibuie today, with its pub, its sea-food smokehouse, its remarkable power of attracting incomers, and its ability to create and stage a play, in the spring of 2003, called *Coigach Riot!* This re-enacted, with many a comic turn and tune on the pipes, the events of 1853, when the crofters of the coast from Badenscallie to Cul-nacraig seized and burned summonses to quit, and beat, abused and humiliated the enforcers until the Clearance was called off.

Coigach is a region apart. As soon as you pass into it, west of Drumrunie, there is an almost palpable pressure from the great rearing mountains and the gulfs between them, which dwarf the isolated settlements and the threads of highway on which they are strung. The land was owned in the middle of the 19th century by a cash-strapped Hay-MacKenzie, heir to the Cromartie estate. She cannily married the future 3rd Duke of Sutherland, grandson of the Black Duke who had cleared Kildonan, Strath Naver, and points north and west. The place feels utterly remote from the cornlands of Cromartie in Easter Ross, or for that matter from the Staffordshire coalfields, railways and canals of the English Midlands where the Leveson-Gowers had amassed their wealth.

It was a time when only a glut of herring staved off serious hunger. Assisted emigration was accepted by many families. They sailed for Tasmania and finally made villages there which mirrored their old clustered townships. At Badenscallie, on the coast that looks west towards the Summer Isles, the crofters were offered resettlement a few miles west along the shore, so that a sheep ranch could be made out of their smallholdings. Out of 93 families 75 undertook to leave. The estate determined to evict the rest.[1] Twice in 1852 the Sheriff's men from Ullapool were met as their boat beached and the writs were burnt. In February 1853 Scorgie Gordon, as his granddaughter Johan MacLeod recalled, ran the twelve miles from Ardmair in two hours, across the Rock, the seaward shoulder of Ben Mor, to warn that another evicting party was on the way. The summonses were found 'nailed under the sole at the stern' and burnt in a bonfire on the beach. The Sheriff's officer was stripped naked for his wintry walk home, giving rise to the story that a pipe tune called *The March of the Cold Testicles* was composed to celebrate the event. (It has never been found. A new tune took its place in the recent play.)[2] Meanwhile a woman called Katie Campbell searched the shoes of the Sheriff's heavies to make sure that no other writs had been hidden there to carry them beyond highwater-mark and so make them count as served. Many women, and men dressed as women, were in the affray. One woman sat in the Sheriff's boat with her hand on the tiller and the boat was carried up the shingle and dumped on top of a potato pit.[3]

This boisterous, almost Rabelaisian reaction to the evictors did not come like a bolt from a clear sky. Coigach had struggled with government and management for generations. Most of the young men had been transported to Virginia and the Carolinas for following Prince Charles Edward Stuart in 1745. In the 1820s there had been evictions from Badentarbat at the north-west end of the chain of townships. The shore cave where a family lived for over a year is still known. Roddie MacLeod of Auchterhouse near Dundee knows that his great-grandfather Murdo was cleared with his family to the rocky island of Tanera Mor in Loch Broom, where the life was 'so horrendous that the family pulled a shutter over it'. A song he has translated, by Neil MacLeod of Polbain where the Tanera people later settled, is eloquent about their anguish:

My curse upon the factors and on the noblemen.
They took our lands away to give to birds and deer.
Today you see only a keeper there, a grey gun in his fist.
Of the land our fathers held we have just the width of our shoe.

The evil that they did to us, deprived of ben and strath.
They drove us to the foreshore, the black headlands of the sea.
Now Weir is in the Parliament, fighting the people's cause,
Demanding they return the land by force they tore away.

Many heroic people whose land was wrenched away
Have gone to Africa and America, far across the sea.
My curse upon the factors who made the hills so hard for us,
That little gang who made us live on the black reefs at sea.

How heartless they are, each earl and duke that was.
They forced away fine heroes, so powerful with their swords.
In battles they were valorous, in wars against the French.
In Waterloo and Corunna they prevailed at length.

Many a healthy family was reduced to poverty –
Miserable, pitiful, friendly, full of warmth and love.
Today nothing but sheep are crying in their place,
And a surly, churlish shepherd, a dog behind his heel.

Look at Badentarbat – it has been made a desert,
Once lived in by crofters, with houses warm and settled.
Where a stranger would get a welcome or a poor man his fill,
Today there are only rushes growing on the meadows.

The pressure of rising population and the desperate resolve of the Cromartie management to make their estate pay squeezed the families beyond endurance. As elsewhere, the women and children used to go the shielings in July and August to give their animals fresh pasture and a chance to yield the winter's keep of cheese and salted butter. Memories survive of the 'happy thoughts' that flourished on these summer sojourns. The shieling at Osgaig, some three miles north-east of Achiltibuie, was 'kindly', being located in a well-watered and wooded valley next to lochs and rivers rich in fish. The

Clach na Conhalaich (stone of the meeting) marks the way that Coigach people took from the coast to the shieling and on eastwards to the fishings, harvests, and religious festivals in Easter Ross. Now such grazings were taken over as pasture for the new big farms. The very shieling huts were forbidden by the estate in case they became permanent dwellings.[6] This merciless policy underlies the extraordinary story, recorded from Morag Shaw MacKenzie in 1982, that the laird's wife in 1820 'found the sight of so many peasant doorways on the Badentarbat hills so obnoxious that she made them turn the doors to the other side of their houses.'[7]

The Coigach rising – a better word than riot – was a fierce ploy that solved little in the short or the medium term. Katie Campbell was forced off the estate and had to build a house with her neighbours' help between the low and high watermarks. By the 1860s, as crops failed in wet summers, the crofters were able to pay only a third of their rents. In the early 1880s they revolted again. The Sheriff's officer who was sent to collect the School Board arrears was driven away – by crofters who could no longer sell their cattle or sheep for a living income.[8] Many people left, for the Lowlands or for New Zealand. Now, in Coigach, out of 261 residents 156 are incomers, many of them English[9] – people whose living no longer has to be won directly from this tough terrain between the abrupt upheavings of the rock and the long reachings of the sea.

Tanera More, Summer Isles, looking towards Achiltibuie and the Assynt hills

Coastal vessels in Badantarbet Bay, off Achiltibuie, with the Assynt and Coigach hills

The Ullapool–Stornoway ferry in Loch Broom

Towards the end of the century-long clearance process, Leckmelm on the flood-plain on the north shore of Loch Broom became a *cause célèbre*. Alexander Pirie, who owned a paper mill in Aberdeen, bought the estate for £19,000 in 1879. Intending to 'convert it into something akin to a Lowland estate', he gave the crofters the choice of being evicted or staying on to work for him. They would have to sell their animals to him and live in rows of new houses. A furious campaign against the deal was carried on by the Free Kirk minister, John MacMillan. The MP for Inverness asked a question in Parliament. The Home Secretary replied that he greatly regretted the clearance–the landowner was of course within his rights.

Most of the crofters accepted Pirie's terms, after at least one brutal eviction. 'On 27th January', wrote a Highland journalist early in 1882, 'I found a substantially built cottage, and a stable at the end of it, unroofed to within three feet of the top on either side, and the whole surroundings a perfect scene of desolation; the thatch, and part of the furniture, including pieces of broken bedsteads, tubs, basins, teapots and various other articles strewn outside. . .The barn in which the infant and wife had to remain all night had the upper part of both gables blown out by the recent storm, and the door was scarcely any protection from the weather. The potatoes, which had been thrown out in showers of snow, were still there, gathered and a little earth put over them by friendly neighbours'–this in the teeth of the fact that local businessmen were asked 'not to employ any longer people who had gone to look on among the crowd'.[1]

The case was discussed at the Napier Commission hearings in Ullapool in the summer of the following year. Those pages of the questions and answers are amongst the clearest definitions of the issues at the core of the Clearances. Fraser MacKintosh, the Inverness MP, asked Pirie, 'Do you think the reducing of the crofters from the status of crofters to labourers dependent upon you is for their benefit?' Pirie answered, 'Certainly, because I think a man who is able to work and make his own livelihood is in a far nobler position than a crofter who every five or six years has to go and cry out, "I am destitute and want help."'[2]

Put in those terms, the landlord's argument is irresistible. Widening the terms, we can think of other forms of landholding, in which one man's say is not all-powerful. John MacMillan, who led the outcry against this clearance, had already advocated club farms to the Commission: 'It is well known that club farms give a greater hold and interest to the people in the lands. There is a union and a unity in such clubs which have a greater power of resistance against high-handed oppression' and that was 'why club farms are so much disliked'[3]–by Pirie, for instance, who told the Commissioners, 'I could have made the whole estate into a co-operative farm, I suppose, but in that case I would never have bought it'.[4]

Co-operation was unlikely in that place at that time. What we see around the head of Loch Broom today is the outcome of clearance and modern farming–no villages, no cottages to speak of and large fields bounded by drystone dykes, some of them probably made from the wrecked homes of the crofters. Neil MacCrimmon, one of the present estate's three full-time workers, was howking boulders out of the ground with two crowbars to plant a fence-post when I went to ask him about traces of the Clearance. He said he had seen old mortar on the stones of some of the field dykes. A former Leckmelm crofter, John MacKenzie, told the Napier Commissioners, 'In the year 1832 every person on the estate was summoned out of his building. . .When the lots were apportioned out among them. . .the people began to clear the stones off the surface of the land, and to improve and cultivate it to make one continuous ground'.[5]

Such was the short-lived crofting township in lower Strath More before Pirie. The consumption heaps they made out of the cleared stones can be seen unforgettably at Inverlael. From the road the steep eastern side of the glen–rather a forced site for a clachan–looks as though a small town has been razed by shelling, bombing, or bulldozing, like Flanders in 1916 or Palestine today. Dozens of house shells mingle with dozens of stone-heaps. The ground is grassiest and clearest in the immediate neighbourhood of each house. Such monuments to handiwork as the treading of boots, the sickling of weeds and the scratching of hens seem to last forever.

All dwellings in this place were made obsolete by Pirie's model housing and steadings, his barns and churn-rooms, kennels and house-rows, which a Commissioner rather nastily called 'barracks'. The plans drawn by Pirie's architect, which still exist in the estate office, are works of art. Glazed windows are rendered in subtle blue watercolour. The kennel railings are like elaborate filigree. Compared with the stubs of home-made cottages left here and there in the encroaching forest, they look like a Fabergé egg contrasted with a clothes-peg whittled by a tinker. You can also find among the spruces a 4-ft cairn which has no obvious use. It isn't on any track a funeral might have followed and it has too few stones to be a consumption heap. Maybe it is a Clearance cairn like one I was shown above Eoligarry in northern Barra. A family built it—a large stone for each parent and a small one for each child—at the point where they got their last sight of the home from which they had been evicted. Maybe some MacKenzie or MacLeod built the Inverlael cairn as they moved, reluctantly and inevitably, down to Pirie's little Utopia.

Beached fishingboat at Morefield, Loch Broom

Loch Broom near Leckmelm

House remains at Leckmelm

INVERNESS-SHIRE

Glen Spean and the hills of the Ardverikie Forest

Autumn in Strath Glass

Strath Glass, a few miles west of Inverness, is perfect. Perfectly beautiful in the long pools of a river translucent and brown as whisky. Perfectly fertile in the lushness of its hay pastures, where the cattle of Iain R. Thompson, author of *Isolation Shepherd*, graze comfortably in winter as well as in summer. Perfectly empty of villages except for the ugly settlement of Cannich, which was cobbled together in a rush to cater for hydro-electric workers in the 1940s and 50s.

Most of Strath Glass was emptied between 1801 and 1831 by the Chisholm chieftain, William, and his wife Elizabeth, daughter of the notorious Marsali Bhinneach, Flighty Marjorie, who had cleared Glen Garry a generation before. The Chisholm tenants emigrated to Nova Scotia, and died by the dozen in the festering ships that sailed from Fort William.[1] Upper Strath Glass was emptied by a rich man from the Borders, Edward Marjoribanks, later Lord Tweedmouth, who bought it for £52,000 in 1854: 'The landscape is very fine; but it was the game that induced me to purchase it.'[2] The view from his vast new mansion at Guisachan would have been spoiled by the clachan of Wester Knockfin, and anyway, he needed its people for his labour force, to mow his lawns and churn his butter, and build a waterfall for the delectation of his guests, and warm his copy of *The Times* and serve afternoon tea to his wife and the guests at their many house parties. So the village and its

neighbours were stripped out and their cottages deroofed. Today you can find a few shells of them between the north bank of the Abhainn Diabhag and the stony track that runs westward towards Affric. Here the women evicted to the model village of Tomich came back every year to lament and keen for their gutted homes.[3]

The headquarters of the clearing class at Guisachan is reached, a mile beyond Tomich, via a drive winding between exotic conifers ninety feet high. Everyone came here once–the future George V and his Queen, the Maharajah of Baroda, Gladstone, Winston Churchill (the nephew of Tweedmouth's son), who learned to drive a car in the grounds, Landseer who gave the title of *Monarch of the Glen* to the chief prey for Tweedmouth and his rifles.[4]

Now between soaring hemlocks and cypresses you see a facade with gaping window-spaces. The fluted cornices sprout a crop of saplings. A notice says 'Danger Private Property Keep Out'. Climbing over the barbed-wire fence, you enter a colossal tottering shell. Wings, stairways, and basements yawn in all directions. Much of the fancy painted and moulded plasterwork still clings to the masonry. Wires encased in slim ducts dangle from the first floor and chatter faintly as they scratch against the walls. They must once have led to a row of bells in the basement, whence the daughters of Tomich would

be summoned to fetch the gentlemen's shaving water or empty the ladies' slops.

The next Tweedmouth in line had spent his fortune and had never much relished the life of a Highland laird, and as a result the estate kept changing hands. By the 1930s the house was a white elephant. In 1938 it was rented by the National Fitness Campaign for Britain's first Keep Fit Summer School. The inmates went in for a good deal of half-naked cavorting and skinny-dipping, to the outrage of Lady Islington at Hilton Lodge just down the river. She bought Guisachan for £1,500, deroofed it and sold the lead and the slates.[5] In the squalor of its dereliction it is now rather less dignified than the poor remnants of Knockfin.

Most of the nine clachans in the main part of the strath have been razed entirely. Their names are still known, from Tigh Cuig, 'place of the bight', to Balmore, 'big settlement', where a few rows of foundation stones still show in the grass. Just one name is still in use, on a map listing the main salmon pools on the river: Arsigon, which is probably garbled from the Gaelic for 'ancient place'.[6] Presumably the evicted people once caught their food in this pellucid pool flanked by white shingle and overhung by broadleaved trees.

In 1831 some of the surviving Chisholms were allowed by the neighbouring laird, Lord Lovat, to settle in Glen Strathfarrar, just over the low hills to the north–which had itself been cleared for sheep in 1803. There was ample room for incomers on the haugh of the Farrar between Loch Beannacharan and Loch a' Mhuillidh. The ruins are not evidence of skilled or careful work. The stones are unshaped boulders and river shingle. There is little trace of ploughing or draining. Perhaps these Chisholms sensed that their time here would not be long. Fourteen years later Lovat cleared them out to make a deer forest,[7] as the

craze for stalking stags and killing them for their meat and their antlers seized the landed class.

This small paradise of a glen winds and winds between high shoulders of mountain until it reaches the source of its water at Loch Monar, a blue serpent fattened now by a majestic concrete dam.

This is the heart of the Highlands. The stands of graceful silver birch, the green pastures between the heathery gorges where the river narrows and deepens, are as eerily pure as an American national park. Strath Farrar is now a Nature Reserve. Notices sponsored by eleven public bodies tell you about the wild deer. Tame ones graze behind the fences of a venison farm. We must sign in when we enter and leave by 5 p.m.—unless we own a section of it, Braulin for example, which is the seasonal toy of a Malaysian shop-owner, 'the wee black mannie'. He flies in for a short blitz on the deer each year and makes his employees sign an oath of secrecy concerning his affairs. His lawns are immaculately mown at all times, his gates are padlocked and he has spent £1 million extending the house in matching local stone.

A former Tory cabinet minister has a place in Strath Glass and Mohammed Fayed, the owner of Harrods, is not far away at Balnagowan. Everyone seems to have a stake in these parts of the Highlands: everyone except the banished Chisholms. There is nobody of that name living in Strath Glass.

The River Glass just upstream from the Arsigon pool

Guisachan House

Glen Strathfarrar: the River Farrar & mountains of West Monar Forest

Coire Dhorrcail, Knoydart

In Knoydart, the mountainous peninsula between Loch Hourn and Loch Nevis in Inverness-shire, there is just one road. It starts at the now thriving village of Inverie and ends eight miles north-west at Airor, which looks to be withering. You can walk into Knoydart by long paths from the east or cross the sea to it by launch or passenger ferry from Mallaig. The oldest inhabitant seems to be Dave Smith, who came here from Kent in 1967. At his croft in Airor, where he was building a wooden calf-pen onto the carcase of an old hay-baler (to cut the cost of transporting his calves to market at Fort William, which consumes a quarter of their value), he pointed to a low stone building nearby with a rusty corrugated roof and said, 'My barn was the house of John MacMaster. He was the only man locally who would help to evict people at the Clearance [in 1853]. And he was put out himself four years later.'

This is the only oral history of the Clearance I have found. It's not surprising that it came from the mouth of an incomer. There are no descendants of the original people living in Knoydart. Contingents of Knoydart people had left for North America in the 18th and early 19th centuries. The land was owned by the spendthrift MacDonells of Glengarry. By the 1840s they were almost bankrupt. The chief's widow, Josephine, and her factor, Alexander Grant, decided to clear the place for a sheep ranch and offered paid passages to the tenant crofters–giving them no time to pay arrears of rent. Four hundred signed on for the voyage, whose destination was changed at the last moment from Australia to Canada. The emigrant boat, *The Sillery*, was anchored off Isle Ornsay, across the sound on Skye. At least sixteen households refused to move, for various reasons.[1] One family had two children with smallpox, in hospital more than a hundred miles away. A wife was pregnant. A widow, Elizabeth Gillies, couldn't face the emigration alone and gave voice to her dilemma with the eloquence typical of a people who have been described by a recent historian as 'largely lacking the ability of fluent self-expression'[2]: 'I am now old, and not able to clear a way in the forests of Canada; and besides, I am unfit for service; and further, I am averse to leave my native country, and rather than leave it, I would much prefer that my grave was opened beside my dear daughter, although I should be buried alive!'[3]

When Grant and his heavies arrived to put her out, 'she sat down beside the fire and would not move an inch'. They extinguished it with water. She then 'struggled hard, seized hold of every post or stone within her reach, taking a death grasp of each to keep possession'. Once they had hauled her outside, 'Stools, chairs, tables, cupboard, spinning-wheel, bed, blankets, dishes, pot, and chest, were thrown out in the gutter. They broke down the partitions, took down the crook from over the fire-place, destroyed the hen roosts, and then beat the hens out through the broad vent [the smoke-hole] in the roof of the house'. The house was then torn down, as were all the houses of those who had left.

We know what happened in such detail because journalists and pamphleteers were now covering the Clearances, notably Donald Ross, a campaigning lawyer. His *The Glengarry Evictions* (1853) dealt with Knoydart, *The Russians of Ross-shire* (1854) with Strath Carron–inland from the Dornoch Firth in Easter Ross–the most brutal, even sadistic of all these events.

Ross has been called melodramatic by a reputable historian.[4] Most of his pages, apart from a few sentences of period atmosphere, consist of eyewitness accounts of how one family home after another was trashed (and one person after another beaten up in Strath Carron): 'the houses, not only of those who went, but of those who remained, were burnt and levelled to the ground. . .Stooks of corn and unlifted potatoes could be seen on all sides. . .[The factor and his men] turned Mac-Dugald and his family adrift, put their bits of furniture out on the field, and in a few minutes levelled their house to the ground. . .The family went back to the ruins of their house, collected some of the stones and turf into something like walls, threw a few cabars across, covered them over with blankets, old sails, and turf',[5] and there they lived until the estate gang destroyed this, too.

The croftlands where all this happened are a deep grassy fringe round the north, west and south shores of the peninsula. They reach deeper into the moor than either a quick trip round or the local map might suggest. Each coastal settlement runs back into the upland along the fertile banks of a burn. Low ridges of ring-dyke built of stone and turf encircle each township. Airor has level field areas which Dave Smith calls his

meadow. At Inverguseran, two miles further north, there is plenty of good grass near the sea and Ian Wilson has a well-equipped farm there. From his meadows, if you look north by west across Skye, you can see Dun Caan on Raasay, rising above Hallaig—a cleared township evoked by Sorley MacLean in his most poignant lyric.[6] It is as though a line were tensed between these two devastated places and it still hums with news and with lament.

Further south on Knoydart are Doune (of which

more later) and Joiner's Croft, where a new family have built an experimental home embodying a black-house which had never been roofed. Croft-house walls still stand in all these places, with more upstream into the moor. Still more stand south of Doune in an unnamed hollow striped with the arable ridges called *feannagan* or lazybeds. This must be Telesaig, which had no people in the 1851 Census and eight by 1861. Presumably it was one of the places where people evicted in 1853 managed to perch for a time. Even more populous is the place north of Airor, beyond the road-end, where the name Niag-ard floats disembodied on the map. This has all the look of a busy township. A series of house-shells on the slope of the hill look down on oblong crofts still outlined by ditches and turf dykes, with grassland near the sea. As Dave Smith put it, 'The good land was near the shore, so they built up on the hill' near sources of stone, well drained, with a breeze to clear the midges. Before the clearance 84 people (12 families) lived here. By 1861 it was deserted.[7]

As you move south from Doune and round the Knoydart headland, you come upon Sandaig: a broad field still machined for hay, one large new house (seldom occupied), and one white-walled cottage near the sea. The new house is on the site of St Anthony's Chapel—'Ruin' in Gothic lettering on older maps. Now the shells of the church and the presbytery have been built up anew with a stone crucifix on the gable as a gesture towards history. The priest here at the Clearance was Coll MacDonald, Maighstir Colla. As the evicted people huddled in their shelters, boiling up a few potatoes, moving again when Grant's men came to tear off their roofs and put out their fires, Coll MacDonald collected blankets and tents, sent urgent letters to Donald Ross, and let homeless people put up their shelters in his garden,[8] now invisible behind dense Leylandii. Forty years later Gillies MacKissock of Inverie, whose family had resisted eviction, recalled that they and other families lived in the tents for three years.[9] The priest's ground was their only sanctuary. The landlord entirely debarred them from the rest of Knoydart.

As you walk the shores and inner glens today you tread ground still green and resilient a century and a half after the people and their animals went away. In spring it is one living embroidery of primroses and violets, celandine and milkwort, with luminous sharp grassblades sprouting through the bleached tangle of last year's growth. This beauty is undercut by a keen awareness that you should be walking past the purple and white of potato flowers and the frosty green of oats. The lazybeds stand out and will stand out forever, often in wine-red stripes where heather has grown down the ridges. At Niag-ard, if you walked along the hill with your eyes shut you would know there had been crofts there because your boots whisk in the heather and bents and squelch on the green runnels in between.

On the north side, high above Loch Hourn, in the mouth of the great corrie on Ladhar Bheinn, you can still see the founds of three shieling huts—circular double layers of stones, six good strides across, on which the women constructed huts of timber and turf. Here they spent summer with the children, making cheese and butter from the milk of the animals they had driven up from the coast. If you climb up there by the glen of the Allt Coire Dhorrcail, you leave the shore near a heathery islet with twin rowans and a level top. Here at the Disruption of 1843 the first Free Kirk services were held, at a time when lairds were refusing to let the breakaway congregations and their ministers get stone and a few square yards of ground on which to build their churches.

This handsome terrain had been hard to live in. The herring deserted Loch Hourn after years of glut. The potatoes were ruined two seasons running by the blight of 1846–7, ample reason for the owners to turn the land over to a product more profitable than human families. What is striking is the zeal with which the managers did their work. When the crofter-fishermen of Arnisdale on the north shore of Loch Hourn asked the factor for house sites further up from the sea, 'he told us then that we should put back-doors upon them, and when the sea came in that we could run away.' This is the sort of fascist wit that was heard everywhere, in Barra, Lewis, Sleat: the bully plumes himself on the cleverness with which he puts down his victim, or uses jeer and bluster to lighten the heinous event.[10]

A hundred and fifty years later it is heartening that decency and civilisation are flowering again in Knoydart. The community has bought a large part of the estate and is running it through a trust which will foster forestry, hydroelectricity, and tourism. The woods are regenerating after fencing and planting by the John Muir Trust on the south coast of Loch Hourn and the place is a glory of new oak and rowan leafage in springtime. At Doune, empty for many generations, the clachan has been reborn in the shape of families spanning the gamut from children to retired people, most of them English. They live in five houses with a boat-building hangar, a timber quay, and a range of wooden-walled holiday cottages, and they run a business based on holiday-making and boating. Now that they have active, happy neighbours once again, the shells of the gutted homesteads look almost peaceful.

Drystone dyke at Airor, with Airor Island and Skye behind

Decaying cottage at Airor, west Knoydart

The north slope of the Knoydart peninsula, Loch Hourn

House at Niag-ard, west Knoydart

Doire na Drise, Arisaig

ARISAIG – INVERNESS-SHIRE

Arisaig, on the road to Mallaig, is now owned by Xavier Namy. 'Who he?' as they say. He is a successor to Lord Cranstoun, who owned and cleared Arisaig between 1829 and 1853. 'I shall never forget the feelings of awe and fear that came over the people of the country,' a Morar man told the Napier Commissioners fifty years after the event.[1] In one case the factor tried to evict a family where a woman lay dead in the house. The people 'seized the functionary, tore his clothes to bits, and soon chased him out of the house.'[2]

Arisaig is comely country, less forbidding and majestic than the seaboards to the north, Knoydart or Torridon or Assynt. Here the shore slopes gently into a shallow sea, then rises again in a garden of reefs and pools and islets where pink thrift grows just above the tidemark. There would seem to be plenty of room in Arisaig and the rolling grassy lowlands just to the north, and the herring and whitefish had always been 'very abundant' in the sea-lochs. The crofters who testified to the Napier Commissioners at Arisaig on 6 August 1883 were desperate for land because so much had been taken from them to make sheep-runs and then a deer forest when what they called 'a mania for sport' took hold in Victorian times.[3] The red deer still flourish and trample the moist watersheds into a mire of cloven hoofprints.

Once when I was exploring the broad headland called Rhu a woman appeared from among the rocks at Port nam Murrach. An aunt of hers called Matheson was from a family who had come into the district with the new railway line from Fort William in 1901. She said, 'We always called the old village along there, south of the forest near Millburn Cottage, Sandaig. And the next one was Gaoideal', which she spelt for me. Gaoideal was once the home of four families, who worked especially good land. It survives on the map as Camas Ghaoideil, its beach. Sandaig is vanishing into oblivion. So is the unnamed group of 'Old Shielings' to its west, presumably Doire na Drise (thorn thicket) which was credited with having had five tenant families in a local mason's evidence to the Deer Forest Commission in 1894. Could our official mappers not have the decency to identify these townships whose names are still known to people, where 79 families lived in at least 12 clachans as recently as the time of our great-grandparents?[4]

The shore of Loch nam Uamh and the Sound of Arisaig is a serration of fiercely folded schists. Caves open black mouths in the rock. One of them near Port a Bhataich has a wall built up in front of it, reminding me of a cave in west Mull which was used for distilling. In another an evicted woman lived for nearly a year before she moved on out of her native place when the people (in the words of a crofter from Back of Keppoch a few miles north) were 'scattered over the wide world; some went abroad and some to Moidart.'[5]

Doire na Drise and Sandaig and Gaoideil occupied fairly level, fairly grassy ground between the sea and the rippling hills of the headland. The ruins of Doire na Drise are houses with five feet of stone courses still standing, thirty feet by fifteen, with corners made from big stones chipped on the round and the wall stones well cut or well split. In one of them I found that rarest of things, a tangible trace of the people who lived here. On the window-sill knives have been sharpened, leaving seven cuts in the grey stone. All the houses, including a surprisingly big one fifty feet long, are next to outcrops and some of these bear signs of artificial cleavage. Obviously the people built next to their quarries, using what a Napier witness called 'native stone close by'. The ground here is fairly wet now. Straight lines mark the course of old ditches. At the shoreward edge of the townland the corduroy of lazybeds is extensive and clear. The whole place receives you with the softening that says 'cradle of civilisation'. The grass is still greener, its stems still juicier than the bents of the surrounding hills.

Sandaig to the east seems barely separate from Torr a Beithe (hill of the birches), once the home of four families.[6] (This name, too, is missing from the map.) It is hillier than the western croftlands, full of sweet grass, and able to offer rooting to a monumental sycamore which grows out of a

ruined house. The highest shell, on a rocky rise, is next to its quarry, a huge flayed whitish slab. Perhaps this was the barn. It has a *toll fhasgnaidh*, a winnowing-hole or low entry in the back wall opposite the main door, so that the wind could blow straight through and separate the flailed ears of oats or barley from the chaff. Young men also used them to creep in to visit their sweethearts.[7] Today the line from the *toll fhasgnaidh* to the doorway leads your eye seaward to Eigg, with its Sgurr standing up in the West Highlands' most distinctive landmark, and beyond that towards America, where so many people from Arisaig and Morar went to look for a more spacious life. Some of them, before they left the Rhu, built a cairn on Cruach Doire 'n Dobhrain (stack of the otters' thicket). They called it 'the Cairn of Greatest Sorrow'. The only thing there now is a concrete triangulation pillar. Presumably the surveyors destroyed the cairn, just as they have banished dozens of cleared settlements from their maps.

Evening light at Doire na Drise

Looking north-west from the Cairn of Greatest Sorrow

Squall over the Sound of Arisaig at Doire na Drise

ARGYLL

The panorama off Ormaig and Cracaig on the south side of Ulva

The River Aline, Morvern

UNNIMORE, MORVERN – ARGYLL

Unnimore is one of the most obscure clearance sites—just one little township in the heart of Morvern, which bulks up between Loch Sunart and the Sound of Mull. What distinguishes the place is the uniquely full and poignant story of how it was cleared, told by one of the evicted tenants, Mary Cameron.

Her village is beside the burn that runs down to Loch Doire nam Mart, half a mile from the track leading north-west from the Strontian to Lochaline road between Claggan and Larachbeg. When I first found it, using a grid reference in Philip Gaskell's *Morvern Transformed*,[1] it was grown over entirely by dense spruce. I managed to count eight shells of houses a few yards from the lush green seam where the Allt an Aoinidh Mhoir pours and falls between banks starred with primroses. The seventy-five people who lived here were cleared by stages in the 1820s at the command of the owner, an unmarried woman who lived in Edinburgh and probably never saw the village she destroyed.

Mary Cameron and her family got work in a cotton mill in Glasgow and there she told her story to the Revd Norman MacLeod, Caraid nan Gal, Friend of the Highlanders, the minister at St Columba's. He worked tirelessly for the 'poor people, or the children of poor people evicted from crofts', who were sometimes 'for a year or two in the lowest state of misery'.[2] Mary's eldest, Donald, died of one of the killer diseases (measles, smallpox) which along with lung troubles like TB attacked the Highlanders who got work in the mills and spent hours 'standing soaked in wet cloth'.[3]

Her incomparable memoir of clearance made two and a half prose pages when it was printed in translation in Norman MacLeod's *Reminiscences of a Highland Parish* (1863). The English is Victorian-literary with its inversions and its 'thou's' and 'art's'. To come as close as possible to a person speaking—without pretending to get back to the Gaelic original—I have turned it into a blank-verse poem in language as natural as possible. Every sentence in Mary's memoir has been retained and only a couple of lines expand slightly on MacLeod's original text.

House at Unnimore below the ridge of An t'Sreang

Unnimore and Beinn na h-Uamha in winter

The Flitting

That was the day of sadness for many of us,
The day Mac Calein* parted with the estate
Of his ancestors—the place of my upbringing.
No-one in Unnimore believed a flitting
Would ever come upon them. While we paid
The rent, which was not difficult, anxiety
Could not come near us. We never asked for a lease.
It was our friendly neighbourhood, we counted
Fifteen smokes between the loch and the hill.
Now there is one—the house of the English shepherd.
Summons to quit arrived. We thought, It is only
A way of raising the rent. We offered that.
They ordered us out at the term. We had to sell
The small cattle whose fleeces I had washed
In the pools of Allt an Aoinidh Mhoir and spread
To bleach on the little loans beside the burn.
At last the cow must go—sold to the factor.
When will I forget the children crying
At their empty bowls? or the last sight I got
Of my crowd of pretty goats on the lip of the crag,
Bleating to be milked? I was not allowed
To put the pail under them. Flitting-day
Had come. The ground officers darkened the door.
When they drowned the fire on the flag of the hearth,
The hissing of it reached into my heart.
We could not get even a bothy in the parish.
There was nothing for it but the land of strangers.
My husband's mother was still alive but crippled.

James put her in a creel and carried her
Strapped to his shoulders. John was at my breast,
Donald and little Mary walking beside me.
Some of our kindly neighbours brought such things
As we could take away, a bench, a stool...
I would feel right if only my heart
Would split, but the relief never came.
We stopped for a last time at the Pass of the Howling
And sat on the Knoll of the Cairns for a last look
At our birthplace. They were stripping it already.
Timbers and thatch were down and the Great Sheep†
Were bleating as the English shepherd's dogs
Chased them into our fields. We were filled with sorrow
But thanks to the Lord above who strengthened us
We did not curse or girn. 'The world is wide,'
James was saying. 'We have nothing to fear,
God will sustain us. Though I have to carry
My mother on my back, and my family
Have not a home in the world, we are as happy
As she who has driven us to this wandering.'

* The Duke of Argyll.
† The *chaora mhor* or Cheviot which was
   now replacing the smaller breeds.

Camus na Croise and the Morvern hills

Camas nan Geall

Nearing Ardnamurchan in the summer, by the ferry from Tobermory in Mull to Mingary Pier at Kilchoan, you notice on the coast a luminous blond plain between the shore and a steep ridge. How can this be–a bare mown hayfield amongst the olive-green pastures and rusty moors, under the lour of Ben Hiant? You are looking at Camus nan Geall (bay of the [monastic] cell) and the townland of Torr na Moine (mound of the peat-moss). More than two hundred bales of hay can be taken from the ground where crofters won their living until they were cleared in the 1820s. Black and brown cattle graze along the track which slants down from the tarred road to the fields next the sea.

Camus nan Geall has extraordinary presence. A track lined with wild flowers divides the 12-acre field, flanked by towering sycamores. Under one of them the tall shaped stones of a chambered burial cairn lean together beside the remains of Cladh Chiarain, once a chapel. Nearer the shingle beach a stone as tall as a person bears on its seaward face a roughly chiselled cross. The stone is probably Bronze Age, the cross a Christian addition. Perhaps it was the work of the Columban missionary Comghan, who was based at Lochalsh and gave his name to Kilchoan and Glencoe. The crofters' monument is a pair of stone buildings at the east end of the beach and at the west end a whole cluster which spreads some

way up grasslands still faintly patterned with lazybeds. As John MacLachlan wrote in his song of about 1830, *Direadh a-mach ri Beinn Shianta*–'Climbing up towards Ben Shiant':

> *So many poor cottages in disarray,*
> *in green ruins on each side,*
> *and houses without a roof*
> *in heaps beside the water-spring*
> *Where the fire and the children were,*
> *that's where the rushes have grown tallest.*[1]

The clearing landowner was Sir James Riddell. He donated supplies of oatmeal, according to the Kirk Session minutes, to help people who were frail, blind, or otherwise helpless, for example in 'the destitution of 1837'.[2] After the Potato Famine of 1846–7, his manager attributed to him 'an aversion to compulsory measures' in reorganising his estate. This may have been bad conscience over the events of twenty years before. In the next township west, Bourblaig, according to Malcolm MacMillan of Carraig at Ardnamurchan Point: 'They shot the dogs, and they shot the goats, and they drove away the cows. And they took the roofs off. It was in wintertime that they did it. And the people walked to Swordle, five miles north, in showers of snow. The wee girl was carrying the riddle for sieving oats. As I understand it, it was a symbol of the future'. Catriona MacMillan of Kilchoan adds the detail (from the granddaughter of

an evicted woman called Henderson), 'Ploughs were put through the potato pits before the houses were torched, so that they would spoil in the frost'. Eilidh MacPhail of Sonachan adds that her husband John's great-grandmother was 'carried out of Bourblaig at the age of six weeks. It did her no harm being carried, she bore eight children, who all reached maturity'.

These stories are the secret history of Ardnamurchan–that is, a past well-known to the people of the place but which has been missing from the printed record. Bourblaig is even physically secret, invisible from the main road and half-an-hour's stiff walk. As you come upon it from the north-east, it opens out into one of the biggest cleared settlements I've seen: at least twenty-six ruins, scattered among a web of turf dykes which will have protected the corn and potatoes from the goats, with the help of juvenile herders–and of course the dogs. In upper Bourblaig these dykes make the best footways, their stone foundations solid, their well-drained tops purple with thyme. Malcolm MacMillan interprets Bourblaig as 'allotment for cattle'. The old way to it was presumably by shore path from Torr na Moine or boat to the sheltered landing called Port 'a Chamais. Abrupt green hummocks frame vistas of the Sound of Mull, south towards Morvern and west to Glen Gorm–said to have been named after the blue smoke of burning roofs.[3] Bourblaig must have

been intensively worked. As you walk back towards the road, you can see how far lazybeds have been pushed up into the steeper, drier ground well south of the houses. On a knoll nearer the main cluster the least sheltered building has a low lin-telled entry in its back wall, surely a winnowing-hole. From the steeps of Ben Hiant (charmed mountain) which looms nearby, a long artery of a cascade pulses down Stallachan Dubha (black cliffs) bringing the clachan its water.

The clearance process here was defined in two sentences by Charles Cameron, a crofter from Acharacle, who testified to the Napier Commis-sioners at Lochaline on 11 August 1883: 'On the north side, where the land is not good, the people are still there; but from the south side, where the land is good, the people were removed. . .They were removed down to the narrow and small places by the shore [Swordle, Ockle, Plocaig, Sanna, Portuairk]; some of them have a cow's grass, and some of them are simply cottars.'[4]

The laird's strong arm was of course the factor. The Sanna writer Alasdair MacLean, one of 20th-century Britain's finest poets, cites two cases of factor power in his classic memoir, *Night Falls on Ardnamurchan*. In 1837 the factor fined two men for 'spoiling a horse's tail', that is, tweaking hairs from an estate animal to make gut for fishing. Next year a Sanna crofter was fined more than the average value of a croft house for 'cutting saplings in the enclosure at Coirevulin. He had been evicted to the north side and had gone back to his old place for wood to roof a shelter for his family.[5] Unsurprisingly the best-known story in West Ardnamurchan, which I first heard in Tobermory fifteen years ago, is about the factor MacColl, who leased the farm of Mingary from the estate. Grass, they say, will never grow on his grave because he was cursed for his heartlessness by a woman he evicted before torching her thatch. The grave in Old Kilchoan Churchyard is certainly without grass, while the plot is surrounded by iron halberds and is almost filled by an engraved stone tablet. Only brambles, nettles, cow-parsley, and goosegrass flourish round it, presumably because the man who scythes the graveyard can't swing his blade inside the fence. MacColl died well before the eviction in Ormsaigmore for which he is still reviled. The legend survives as an epitome of the passionate grievance which crofters felt towards any factor.

> *... the living-room and the other room,*
> *The closet and the potato-bunker,*
> *Are all covered with the rushes*
> *That sprout from the urine of the white-faced sheep.*[6]

These accurate lines were written in the 1880s by Gillean Currie, brother of the postman who worked from Lochaline in Morvern. Many laments were written by the bards of western Argyll for what had happened in their forebears' country. The displaced people, those forced out and those who chose to leave, sailed by the thousand from the Relief Pier at Lochaline. It was built in the 1840s by the men, women, and children of the district for a 'wage' of 14 lb of meal a week per man (10 lb per woman; children according to age). The information board at the pier has these lines:

> *Guid chaidh that cuan,*
> *cuid s'a chill ud shuas*
> *'S cuid cha'n ed fhios caite*

> *Some went over the ocean,*
> *some to the graveyard*
> *Where the others are no-one knows*

In this land so marked by emigration it was both heartening and poignant to hear from Joan Matheson of Kilmory about a Bourblaig family who moved out to New Zealand, after some years in the transit camps of Ockle and Swordle, and did well there. She herself is the great-great-niece of factor MacColl and almost apologised for her notorious relative. The MacKenzies she told me about had been active in the 'Forty-five. The uncle of the Hugh MacKenzie who emigrated had impersonated Prince Charlie to help him escape, and had then been shot by an army patrol. The family were heavily fined after Culloden and emigrated three generations later, in 1839. In the North Island of New Zealand they helped a Morvern man to establish the sheep and cattle industry of the country, in the broad and well-watered vale of the Wairarapa. The Rimutaka range separates Wellington and the Hutt valley from this pioneer land to the north. Here MacKenzie's son John, born at Achateny near Kilmory, took the trouble to learn Maori and was given *tapu* (immunity) by the Maori in their final war against the British colonists. He married a woman he met as he led a party of people and animals across the mountains by a bridle path where the road now climbs and falls by hairpin bends through dense forest.

On the far side, where the rich grasslands make perfect farming country, the Ruamahanga River runs down to a lagoon and a colossal rampart of shingle. The breakers throbbing in from the Pacific mesmerise you as they arch and burst in a stramash of ice-green and Antarctic white. As you look out to the far edge of the seemingly infinite plain of water, it seems more extraordinary than ever that people from the westernmost point of the Scottish mainland should have colonised this last piece of 'free' land and learned to cohabit with its people, for both ill and good.

Bourblaig, looking towards Loch Sunart and the hills of Mull

Detail of house at Bourblaig

House at Bourblaig, with Ben Hiant, in winter

The Clark family graveyard, Ulva

ULVA – ARGYLL

On the run across to Ulva from Mull the ferryman's 8-year-old daughter, from one of the very few families living on this fertile island that once exported potatoes, stands up on the gunwale, gets her fingers over the rim of the deckhouse, and swings along for a foot or two. Then she drops onto the deck and grins quickly round, wanting us to be pleased with her daring. So, no doubt, the island children would have played, until eviction and the Potato Famine exhausted them.

Ulva is Wolf Island, *Ulffur*, from the Norse. The last wolf on Ulva was F.W. Clark, a lawyer from Stirling. He bought Ulva in 1835, hoping for good profits from kelp-making. When this industry failed nation-wide, he began to clear the island of its people. The population fell from 604 just before the first Census in 1841 to about 150 in 1851, a few years after the potatoes rotted. On 13 February of that year Clark testified to the Board of Supervision of the West Highlands & Islands in terms that define the classic landlord position: 'Finding that the crofters could not pay their rents, and that my private resources were therefore diminished from year to year, I had no alternative but either surrender my property to the people or resume the natural possession of the land'.[1] A dilemma indeed. Some may well think that 'natural possession' belongs more properly with 'the people' than with the speaker of those words.

Two stone-built works that have survived on Ulva typify the place. One is the house of a cleared family at Ormaig near the south coast (seven families evicted).[2] It stands six feet high, well-masoned with rounded corners, clear of the coarse green bracken foliage which Sorley MacLean, the Raasay poet, saw as the curse which comes over the land after clearance. This village was where the MacArthurs had a piping school, reputed to be the equal of the more famous MacCrimmons of Skye. From here a path leads westward parallel to the shore. Your feet, invisible below you through the tangled fronds, are following a trod so firmly beaten that it must have been the main thoroughfare hereabouts. Two boulders flank the path and you realise you're leaving Ormaig through the gap in the ringdyke and entering the outby land between Ormaig and the next township, Cracaig ('cupped-hands hollow'): nine families evicted.[3] The worked land here is roomy, with many stripings of lazybed and ditch. An easy, shingly landing-place opens out between the grotesque basalt crags of the shore. An outcrop good for building materials shelters the place to the north. The only animals grazing the pasture are deer, who hide expertly behind copses of saughs and hazel.

Lachian MacQuarie, a shoemaker, once a crofter and lobster fisherman, was evicted from Ormaig to Cracaig, then 'In a short time again he was warned out of there also, and on refusing to leave his house was stripped by a policeman and a sheriff officer along with the proprietor and some working men. Being then homeless, having a wife and three young children, he had to take the couples (being his own) that were on the house, carry them to the shore, and put up a hut for himself there, about six yards above the high-water mark.' This description of the evictions is part of a group testimony to Napier at Tobermory on 10 August 1883. The men's evidence is incomparably full and detailed. They remembered Clark 'closing up with stones the only good well near him', smashing a kettle near the well, tearing up clothes bleaching by the roadside, pulling up saplings which people had planted to make their new homesteads less bare, stripping the roofs off huts, leaving a small piece above the head of a very sick woman... It all sounds like the inverted rage that a tormentor turns on a victim, as he tries to blind himself to the atrocity he's committing.

This terrible record helps to explain the poisonous aura surrounding Clark's remains. It was said that when the tombstone imported for his grave was brought ashore from the ferry, it could not be moved further 'because of the weight of the evil that was in it'. When at last the waggon approached the burial ground at the south-east end of the island, the horses became mired. The slab was unloaded and at once sank into the moss,

where it still lies. If this is true, the family must have sent for another one, since the biggest stone in the graveyard is inscribed for both Clark (died 1887) and his wife Agnes Wright who 'fell asleep in Jesus' in 1859, a woman 'whose amiable disposition and Christian virtues shone forth so conspicuously'. Other slabs commemorate three daughters, and a son who became Sheriff of Lanarkshire. As the ferryman said to me grimly, 'He must have sent a few down.' To reach this last resting-place of the Clark dynasty you have first to locate it among the boggy dales and heathery hillocks in that corner of the island, where it stands on a knoll looking out superbly across Loch na Keal to the headland of Ardmeanach on Mull. Then you have to do a short rock-climb. The graveyard is girt all round by crags, and the wall surrounding the little circle of nettles, thistles, and gravestones has no way in. In this it contrasts with the good houses at Ormaig and Cracaig, whose doorways stand forever open.

The mill-house, Cracaig

The church at Scalasaig

COLONSAY – ARGYLL

Colonsay, south of Mull and west of Jura, feels like a favoured island, compared with say Eriskay or North Uist. Belts of good grass wind round the crags. Corncrakes grate from coverts amongst the hay and even scurry through people's gardens. Oaks and birches cluster thickly in sheltered places.

Oronsay, the next island south, which you can walk across to at low tide, was the plinth for an Augustan priory. Here masons and stone-carvers created works of classical beauty, tombstones alive with antlered deer and fully rigged sail-boats, within yards of the gradual shore celebrated by Donald MacNeill, Colonsay's chief modern bard (he died in 1995):

> Orasa nan traighean grinneal,
> Traighean grinneal mm gan sluaisreadh,
> Stuadhantan ur bho uchd a chuain
> Bualadh fuaimneach mar o chionn. . .
>
> Oronsay of the sandy beaches,
> beaches of fine sand sifted by the waves,
> breakers fresh from the breast of the ocean,
> crashing loudly as they always did...[1]

The naturalists of the Hebrides, Darling and Boyd, rejoice that 'these islands are in the possession of one who recognises their value and beauty in the natural history of the west'[2]–that is, Lord Strathcona and his son Alexander Howard. Although they have sold Oronsay to a Mrs Colburn of Boston, who alights there for a month in the summer and pays heavily to have it exquisitely manicured, Colonsay is certainly well-managed, with plenty of cattle and adequate tourist accommodation–owned almost exclusively by the laird. This is in a long tradition of monopoly. When a mill was set up at Kiloran in the 1830s, people were forced to take their oats there to be ground. Many people secretly kept their querns, which came in handy for grinding hand-outs of maize during the Potato Famine.[3]

The old lairds, too, had a reputation for caring, especially in the eyes of the canny minister who wrote the island's entry in the *Old Statistical Account* (1791–9). He scolded his flock for preferring the imagined fleshpots of America to hard work on Colonsay. Most emigration from the island, which was heavy early in the 19th century and again after the Famine, seems to have been more or less voluntary, undertaken by people who had saved up to go. An exception was a contingent who passed through Islay in 1791, possibly on their way to Australia. The customs officer, Malcolm Campbell, described them as 'passengers with all their effects, which consist only of wearing apparel, as they are poor labouring people who have been deprived of their farms by their landlord.'[4]

The present-day historian of Colonsay, the scholar, pier-master, and school-bus driver Kevin Byrne, believes that these people came from the neighbourhood of Beinn a' Tuath (north hill), between Kilchattan and Urugaig. The burn there is called Abhainn nan Toiteanan (stream of the ruins). Southward from it, on the heathery eastern slope of the hill, there runs a chain of white-stone cottage shells, perhaps six dwellings altogether, with built-on barns or byres. The gables are eight feet high, with no sign of flues. Presumably the fires were in the centre of the floor. The most upstanding of the buildings has a walled field in front of it, perhaps a kailyard. The 20-ft square of it still shows as a stone outline in the turf. All that grows there now is a small yellow blaze of trefoil at one corner and a few peculiarly pale violets round an outcrop in the middle.

The story of a high-handed clearance by a MacNeill laird is told on the island–the story of 'how the Bells left Balnahard', which is the northernmost tilled and grazed land, now a farm. 'There were a lot of them living up there and they were in a dispute about the division of the land. They couldn't agree, so they went in a deputation to the big house. The laird said to them, "What can I do?" "It is this way, my lord. We cannot agree about the lands we have. Now, can you adjudicate amongst us?" "I will need to think about this. Come here again this day week and I will tell you what to do." So they came there the next week, on the same day, and he says to them, "Right, my men, I have considered what you must do. Go you home now and pack your traps, you are leaving tomorrow on a boat from America." And that is what they did, they left from the beach in Balnahard.'[5]

This must be a myth—a story whose meaning is oblique, not literal. I suggest that the earlier clearance via Islay had left a taint of grievance. The Bells (and others) in fact left in good order in 1806, on one of seven boats which sailed for the Canadian Maritimes from Oban and Tobermory. You can see the graves of many of these folk in Woods Island Pioneer Cemetery, in a dell amongst spruces and aspens, near Belfast on Prince Edward Island.[6]

The tacksmen or substantial tenants on many Hebridean islands could see the writing on the wall. What it said was that the lairds were bent on building a modern economy with little room for the smaller and less profitable tenants.

On Colonsay several good-sized farms were made out of the best land in the middle of the island and let to incomers. Instrumental to such reorganisation was the laird's manager, the factor, often a farmer in his own right who could manage the dispossessions to his own profit, the selling-off of stock and the reallocation of crofts. Always a figure of grudge and even hate, he is remembered in Colonsay in a story told me by Donald

Gibbie MacNeill, a white-haired calmly-spoken crofter whose family have been on the island since records began. He had been scything in his garden, which is an oasis of flowers surrounded by the rough pasture of his croft at Baile Iochdraich (lower homestead). 'I know an old fellow', he said, 'he is dead a long time and his family had to spin flax in payment of a part of their rent. They might have been doing as much as a day and a half's work to pay their rent. It was mainly the women who did that work. This fellow's wife was just at death's door at the time, so he asked that his wife might not have to do it. This factor said, "We must have the work done." So the man spun the flax into a ball—into a tangled mass, like a ball of

rope, and he said to the factor, "If you don't want it like that, you won't get it."'

The other removal on Colonsay which has the bad odour of clearance is the transfer of the people from Riag Buidh, north of Scalasaig where the ferry puts in. They lived on what was perhaps the last runrig clachan in the Highlands, with common fields which were reapportioned each year. After the Great War, when 'homes fit for heroes' were being built by many councils, the Riag Buidhe people were moved a little south to Glas Ard. Their thatched roofs were burnt in short order. Valuables stored in the roofs, such as spinning wheels, were destroyed. What Kevin Byrne regrets about the constant departure of Colonsay people from their homesteads is another sort of loss: 'They went mob-handed [early in the 19th century], babes-in-arms and grandmothers, everybody. They took with them the knowledge of Colonsay, and now nobody knows the meaning of many of the place-names'.

The Kilchattan road, Colonsay

The east side of Beinn a' Tuath, with the hills of Jura

House on the west side of Beinn a' Tuath

The township of Tarskavaig, with the Cuillins and the Red Hills

Private chapel at Raasay House

The dead have been seen alive. This line from Sorley MacLean's poem about the township of Hallaig, on the east coast of Raasay, distils the lasting essence, the surviving memory, of the Clearances. Humankind might still be there, among the stonework half-immersed in nettles and bracken, the ridges of the lazybeds where crops once grew... but no, they've gone. The poet was thinking of the young women of the past generations in Hallaig. He caught sight of them in the woods between the crofts and the sea-cliffs:

... na h-igheanan 'nan coille bheithe,
direach an druim, crom an ceann.

... the girls a wood of birches,
straight their backs, bent their heads.[1]

And there they are today, the brown-and-silver ghosts. No, they are sturdier than that, they have withstood centuries of sea-winds scathing across the Inner Sound between Raasay and Applecross on the mainland.

They will have been an invaluable resource for the Hallaig people, yielding twigs for besom-brooms and thicker wood for handles for the *cas chrom*, the foot-plough. In Diabaig in Wester Ross, about 1963, I was with Murdo MacKenzie when he went with his axe into the birchwood behind his croft, cut down a sapling with the right curves in its trunk, and fashioned it into a handle for the plough with which he later dug his potato field. All four sides of Sorley Maclean's family were evicted from one Raasay township after another, and this was typical. Expecting eviction, one man went over to his brother-in-law's croft on Skye to plant his year's potatoes. Another was put out of his home although he had been a piper whose hands were frostbitten in the Peninsular War.[2] And so on. As Raasay became overcrowded (834 people in 1851), dozens of families accepted help from the owner to emigrate to Prince Edward Island or Australia. Dozens who stayed were cleared forcibly to make room for sheep-farms. It happened in waves throughout the 1830s, '40s, and '50s.[3] It happened in Hallaig and Screapadal, in Fearns and Leac and Suishnish, until 'It is not soil, but rocks we are occupying' and 'It was all animals to the south, people to the north,' in the words of one crofter in the 1890s and another a few years ago.[4] When people were forced out, they carried as mementoes handfuls of the grass and soil that had covered the graves of their kinsfolk[5]—a last despairing version of the *fad seilbh*, the 'turf of ownership' traditionally given when land changed hands.

The green south end of the island and the rocky north are linked on the west side by a road that was built by one man, Calum MacLeod, and completed thirty years ago. On the east side the way leads north from Hallaig by wavering sheep-trods through woods of rowan and birch, under grotesquely layered white and yellow crags, over the greens of the emptied townships. In spring it is lit by constellations of primroses. This is perhaps the most beautiful walk in the Western Isles—if you can bear what Sorley called 'the heartbreak of the tale'. As you reach the township of Screapadal, three and a half miles north of Hallaig, your footsoles feel the tenderness of ground that was tilled and dunged for generations. It is 'fine green grassy ground', in the words of John MacLeod, a crofter who testified in Gaelic to the Deer Forest Commission in 1893.[6] People from thereabouts had loved the beauty of the place. They loved to hear the grouse and the cockerels, the cows and the dogs, when their calls were carrying across the sea from Applecross—as did the lament of a mother for her son, the legendary Raasay hero Faobairne MacCuidhein, who was shot dead on the beach by the arrows of raiders.

Seventeen families lived in Screapadal in 1841. I count 36 ruins there today, which presumably include kilns and keep-houses as well as dwellings. In Sorley MacLean's words,

Da fhag Reanaidh Screapadal gun daoine,
gun taighean, gun chrodh, ach caoraich,
ach da fhag e Screapadal boidheach;
R'a linn cha b'urrainn dha a chaochladh.

Rainy* left Screapadal without people,
with no houses or cattle, only sheep,
but he left Screapadal beautiful;
in his time he could do nothing else.[7]

As so often in the croftlands, the old lived-in place is girt by a ring-dyke, a wide-looping low

structure made of a course of boulders crowned with turfs, on which heather, tormentil and bent-grass grow now. 'It was not a fortress wall that encapsulated the community, not a dividing line, but a link between the elements of the township. As soon as the crops were off the ground, the dykes were breached, and the stock were free to roam on the townland, which now became common gazing too... The date for opening the dykes was not precisely fixed, and would vary with the state of the weather and the date of harvest, but [it] was a strong incentive to the slower tenants to get their crops off the ground and into the stackyard at the same time as their neighbours.'[8]

By mainland standards there is not much room for cultivation on the steep land inside the dyke at Screapadal. In the opinion of John MacLeod a century ago there was enough room for four families.[9] As a result of the clearance there are none. The long alp of Screapadal, stretching from the mess of felled spruce plantation in the north to the white and yellow cliffs of Creag na Bruaich, the 'border rock', in the south, is one of the most eloquent monuments to the old culture of the Highlands and Islands.

*The sugar trader who bought Raasay in 1846

'A wood of birches' – approaching Hallaig from the south

Hallaig: post-clearance barn and wall below Dun Caan

Hallaig, looking across the Inner Sound to Applecross

'Jungle' north of Screapadal

Screapadal under the crags of Creag na Bruaich

Basalt formation in Glen Uig

For Sorley MacLean Skye was 'eoin mhoir sgiamhach na h' Albainn', 'the great beautiful bird of Scotland', lying on the sea with her 'supremely beautiful wings bent about many-nooked Loch Bracadale'.[1] Trotternish is the final, most northerly of her four plumes. In the 1880s they stirred again at last and buoyed the island up in its belated fight against doubled rents, evictions and poverty.

Kilmuir, at the north-west corner, is a broad shelf of fertile land between a craggy hill ridge and the sea. By the 1880s its crofts, rarely of more than two acres, were yielding little more than twice the weight of sown oats. Much of the land had been turned over to large sheep-farms and the crofters had lost the rights to pasture their animals on the hill. The farms surrounded them 'so that we have no escape on either side, as if we were shut up in a fold'.[2] Most families shared their houses with their cows. Sooty water dripping through the thatch sometimes forced them to sleep outside. They were not even allowed, according to John MacDonald of Solitote near Duntulm, 'the privilege to cut heather for binding the roofs of our houses, or rushes to thatch them with' unless they gave some days' work to the farmer.[3] For bedding, people were using whelk or flour bags, which they unstitched, bleached, and sewed up again.[4] You might think that the fruits of the unchartered sea, planted by nobody, would be owned by nobody. The crofters were prevented from gathering mussels for bait and had to buy seaweed from the landowner or his farmer tenants to manure their fields.[5] Without the horses they had pastured on the hill, they were reduced to carrying seaweed in creels on their own backs and to dragging harrows with the traces over their own shoulders.[6]

Unbearable poverty bred revolt. Militant phrases spark out from the testimony given to the Napier Commissioners. A crofter told them at Skeabost, at the head of Loch Snizort: 'As the Gaelic proverb says, "It is about time that the bellows worked."' Another man told them at Stenscholl on the east coast, 'After hearing of good news from Ireland [about anti-landlord actions], we were much inclined to turn rebel ourselves'.[7]

Many of the Trotternish grievances were embodied in the owner, Captain Fraser from the Black Isle, and his factor, Alex MacDonald. Fraser's Skye base, a mile from the modern ferry terminal, was in what a crofter called the 'beautiful glen' of Uig.[8] The weird basalt crags that flank its green length like forts sit on a layer of Oxford clay. By 14 October 1877 this had been saturated with rain and it bulged outwards, undermining the rock. Millions of tons avalanched down the glen, destroying Fraser's big house and gardens and the graveyard. If you walk up the river from the shore, you can still find squared stones in the undergrowth. Coffins burst open or were carried out to sea and lost. 'The dead body of Captain Fraser's evicted crofter' was 'deposited in the dining-room', or so said the local correspondent of The Highlander, which was fined £50 for describing the flood as 'a judgement for Captain Fraser's cruelty to his tenants'.[9] The disaster was fairly impartial, however, since the crofters' fields were also buried deep in debris and the families had to rummage in it for their potatoes.

A Napier witness called the estate's policy of constantly moving tenants from one place to another 'a shaking of the people' which is 'next door to evictions'.[10] Eviction was often outright. The most detailed testimony comes from Donald Nicolson of Solitote, formerly of Totescore, which the estate wanted to absorb into the big farm of Monkstadt. (Monkstadt big house is now a gaunt ruin like something from a horror film, and the cottages and massive steadings nearby look eerily under-used.) Nicolson's rent was doubled with an extra £1 on top of that. When he refused to pay the extra pound, he was locked out of his own house and his neighbours were warned against helping him, on pain of eviction the following year. 'The peats were locked up... We had not the fire to prepare a cake.' His wife and children had to sleep in the stable and 'I myself was sleeping on the stones.'

His evidence concludes: 'My family was scattered when I lost the place.'[11] Across Loch Snizort in Waternish, Alan Beaton can remember his father telling him how as a child he sheltered in an open drain with his mother when the Dunvegan factor torched their house to force them out.

By the end of 1884 Trotternish and Waternish were seething with revolt. Meetings of between three hundred and a thousand crofters assembled at the Quiraing,[12] summoned by the Dudach Mhor, the great horn—perhaps the very one you can see in the Museum of Island Life at Hungladder.

In the Quiraing itself pinnacles of volcanic conglomerate tower on the slopes of the mountain like gigantic firs or emaciated ogres. Black gullies ooze and collapse between the spires. In their midst is the natural platform called The Table, an acre of perfect grassland, smooth and tilted slightly southward. There could be no better arena for a mass meeting, secret, hugely atmospheric and comfortable—once you have climbed steeply up to it by a labyrinth of paths. Locals believe that the meetings were probably held on the easier ground at the bealach, where there is now a car park. This was on the customary route from east to west, used, for example, by Staffin people to take their horses to the good pastures at Lianacro for a few months.

The crofters attending the meeting resolved to stop paying rent and to demand the replacement of factor MacDonald. Their rulers reacted to the crofters' militancy by sending small battleships and squads of marines to intimidate the people and guard the sheriff's men as they served their summonses.[13] This stage in the Crofters' War is vividly remembered in Kilmuir and Staffin.

Norman Stewart of Valtos, nicknamed Parnell after the Irish leader, had been imprisoned for taking heather and rushes to thatch his house. Now he became a leading light in the campaign to withold rents and resist summonses for arrears. His long face with its high cheekbones and grizzled beard gazes with formidable authority from a photograph in Iain Fraser Grigor's *Mightier Than a Lord*—although, as his grandson pointed out to me, the caption wrongly names him 'John'.[14] His brother Calum is remembered as a fellow militant. According to Lachie Gillies, fisherman from Stenscholl, 'He had a stick in his hand, and when the sheriff officers came in their gig, he lifted it and broke the five fingers of the man's hand'. The rank-and-file marines were not seen as part of the estate and its military allies and were hospitably treated in their billets, although the Skye folk and the Lowland soldiers could not understand each other's languages. Today, as you look down between the gnarled spires of the Quiraing, the Staffin crofts show vivid green with fresh aftermath or luminous yellow where the hay has just been mown and gathered. In the west the broad fields of Kilmuir are well populated with black cattle—an unusual sight these days in the islands, although I remember it as commonplace on Skye in the 1950s. Feaull was one of seven empty crofts claimed in a protest song of the 1880s, still sung in Kilmuir in 1973. Nowadays a brown bull minds his cows there and turns his blunt muzzle and curly pow to face you as you walk past. This degree of prosperity is what the crofters won by their battles a hundred and twenty years ago. In 1904 the Congested Districts Board bought Kilmuir and a few years later the Department of Agriculture became the owner, which it still is—'a good landlord', as it was put to me. After twenty-five years of public ownership the tilled acreage had risen by a third, the crofters' total acreage by a half, ten large farms had gone, 85 new crofts had been created, and 288 holdings had been enlarged.[15] How much of this would have happened had it not been for the likes of Mrs MacMillan of Heribusta, just north of Feaull? She is remembered as 'a strong big woman' who pelted the police with dung when they came with summonses. She was arrested, then released when the sheriff found she was pregnant. The site of her house, now occupied by a new barn, is still known to the people of Hungladder and Kilvaxter.

House at Feaull, looking towards the township of Kilmuir.

Croft at Valtos in eastern Trotternish

Cattle near Torvaig, Trotternish

The crags of the Quiraing, with The Table, centre-left

House-wall and basalt crags at Feaull

Loch Harport at Gesto, looking south

TUASDALE – ISLE OF SKYE

The young woman on the quad-bike had used an amazing phrase about Tuasdale—she called it 'the capital of Skye'. The following year her parents, Willy and Oonagh MacPherson, who farm at the head of Loch Eynort in Minginish, western Skye, used the same phrase. So did John MacDiarmid, on his tractor at the modern steading up the hill. The place itself, between Talisker Bay and Glen Brittle, is 'Tusdale' on the latest map. It is 'Tuasdale' in Nicolson's history of Skye, published in 1930. This agrees with the MacPhersons' pronunciation and presumably means 'north glen'. In the Napier evidence taken at Bracadale in 1883 it is 'Duisdale'.[1] On the map there are no hollow squares to denote old buildings—simply the name.

To reach it you can either climb straight over the ridge north of the road-end at the head of Loch Eynort, passing through the Bealach na Croiche, or else take a path parallel to the shore between Beinn Buidhe na Creige (yellow hill of the sunlight) and Biod na Fionaich (point of the whiting). By either way you enter a broad, long, gently-expanding green basin with two burns that meet in a 'Y' and flow heartily towards the sea. One human remnant after another springs into focus. House after house still stands, dozens of them in three clachans, many with well-masoned walls six feet high, the external corners rounded. Some stand singly, some are huddled so close that there are alleys between them. Some are double—a family space with a separated byre? Some are free-standing and little—kilns for parching barley? One has a wing at right angles to the main building. One is so near the Tuasdale Burn that its corner has been torn off by a spate. The more huddled houses are built in a way we have seen nowhere else: the outer walls are ramparts of rubbly stone, as much as eight feet thick.

Nobody has lived in these houses since 1840. Near the head of the townland a two-storey ruin with curiously narrow, pointed windows stands up like a gawky carcase. This was Borlin Lodge, named after one of the cleared clachans, a big township in which there were twelve families.[2] Nobody has lived in it since 1910. The last man to spend nights hereabouts was Donald Ferguson, a shepherd now aged 93, who lives in Carbost, three miles over the hill. For many years before the Second World War he slept in a bothy beside the lodge at lambing time. He remembers the loch as being 'full of seals and otters'.

Every slope of the ground round Tuasdale is striped with lazybeds, thousands of them. When the bracken flourishing on the ridges withers in October, they show up as bronze stripes on the green hillsides. Seaward of the clachans, on the western slope of the dale, there is a huge field 700 yards long and 150 across, which the MacPhersons call 'the stone park'. This is the usual stigma of clearance, branded onto the land by the farmer who took over the gutted crofts.

As you walk from house to house, with Canna in full view out to sea, you feel in the midst of activity. The burns have been embanked with stonework. The path round the shoulder of Beinn Buidhe na Creige is palisaded on its downhill side. The houses put on roofs again as you look; there are children minding the cattle, standing guard on the ring-dykes which mesh the slopes. Women are milking in the open with their three-legged stools, horses are whinnying to each other, the men newsing as they dig, about the French wars or the latest scandal concerning the MacLeods of Dunvegan or the MacCaskills of Talisker.

Twelve families were evicted from 'Duisdale' about 1840.[3] They had been living 'in comfortable circumstances'. The whole place was cleared by the tacksmen under the MacLeod landlord, first by Dr Lachlan MacLean, who also cleared Rum,[4] and then by Hugh MacCaskill. This was called 'the Reign of Terror', according to the Napier witness Alexander Mathieson of Carbost.[5] MacLean was also noted for his habit of having a sheep's ears cut off close to the skull when it was impounded, to be sure of identifying the animal if it strayed again.

Pointing up the hill from their back door, the MacPhersons said, 'Do you see that ruin?' It stands on Cnoc Loisgte, 'hillock of the burning'. 'When they put the woman out who was living there, they put a match to her roof, and her stock of butter and cheese was running down the hill. And that was her winter's keep.' This is how the American army treated the food-stores of the Ojibwa, around the same time and for much the same reasons.

MacCaskills and Macleods are handsomely commemorated in the church and chapel on the shore of Loch Eynort, two roofless buildings standing beside each other in a graveyard dappled by the shadows of broad-leaved trees. The various MacCaskill monuments, burials from the 1770s to the 1960s, are lying about in a litter of carved granite inside a rusted iron fence with points like halberds. On the headland of Faolain nearby, a fishing station with slated roof and net-drying poles looks out over the sea-loch where the men of Eynort used to catch their white-fish. The south shore between Grula (five families evicted) and Kraiknish (sixteen families evicted)

has been smothered in industrial spruce. The forestry men used to feel uneasy at working amongst the ruins there 'because there was a powerful atmosphere'.

When the people here call Eynort and Tuasdale the capital of Skye, in a way that seems both ironical and heartfelt, they are being proud about the complete sub-culture that once flourished here. This was the heart of Minginish, the wing of Skye bounded by Glen Sligachan to the east and Loch Harport to the north. In his epic lament *An Cullithionn – The Cuillin*, Sorley MacLean calls it:

Minginish of the abundant breast,
soft Bracadale of the lovely pap hollows,
washed by the hidden kiss of the sea...
Minginish of most graceful slopes,
of greenest bushes...
Minginish gathering into a fold
Waternish and Sleat...

The acute black sgurrs of the Cuillin are only a few miles from Tuasdale across Loch Eynort. Their towering fierce beauty is tragic to MacLean because of the ravaging that happened here in the 19th century:

It is that they rise
from the miserable torn depths
that puts their burden on the mountains.

Because we know this history, we cannot help seeing

the great Island in its storm-showers
as seen by the homesick eye
that looked on America while it desired Grula...[6]

Houses at Tuasdale, with lazybeds on the slopes of Beinn na Cuinneag

Borlin Lodge, Tuasdale

Last vestiges of a house at Tuasdale, looking to Borlin Lodge

Standing-stone at Boreraig

Boreraig on the shore of Loch Eishort in south-west Skye is a cradle of the culture which suffered severely under the sheep-farming policy of the MacDonald Lords of Sleat. When you find out exactly how Boreraig and its western neighbour, Suishnish, were cleared under the supervision of a factor called Ballingall, you can see why Sorley MacLean placed him in a fiendish chorus on the summits of the Cuillin:

On every pinnacle of the Cuillin
the image of a spoiler was rocking. . .
contemplating the Minginish they had shorn.
East, on the skyline of Sgurr nan Gillean
there rose the likeness of Major Fraser,
and on their hunkers on the Bidean
were Ballingall and Mr Gibbon. . .
And in all the corries below
every slick fawner of their band,
every factor, lawyer and gent
who ate and licked around,
who dragged and plundered and drove.[1]

Ten Boreraig families were warned out in 1850 and sent to Australia on the *Hercules*. In Heast, the next village to the east, they still recall how the brother of one of the evicted men went up the hill to Coire Buidhe, which gave a view of Broadford Bay, to see if the ship was still at anchor or had carried his brother away forever. A further batch were warned out a year later and the remainder in the autumn of 1853, including a widow aged 96. Her grandchildren tried to feed her 'with warm milk and some bread from a neighbour's house as if she had been a pet bird'. The estate men were throwing the furniture out of the houses and nailing bars across the doorways. The widow, Flora Matheson, half-walked, half-crawled to a byre without door, window, or bed. When her son came home months later and lodged with her and his children, he fell ill and died within weeks. He lay with his feet against the back wall and his head in the doorway: 'The wind waved his long black hair to and fro until he was placed in his coffin.'[2]

Because many of the cleared moved a few miles east onto cramped, poor land for which Lord MacDonald had no use, their descendants are still there, with family memories still clear in their minds. Alastair MacKinnon, postman at Sasaig on the other side of Sleat, told me how he heard from his grandmother about her flight along Loch Eishort-side towards Drumfearn. They spent the night there in the open: 'Her eyes shed more tears than she received milk from the cows.' Neil MacKinnon, lobster fisherman at Heast, told me that he had heard via his maternal great-grandmother, a MacInnes, how the estate heavies treated a family called Kelly, who lived next to the waterfall that bounds Boreraig to the east. There were baby twins in the family. 'They were not clearing them en masse, it was one at a time, so the people did not know what was going on. When the estate men came to the house they asked for a drink of water, and she was going to give them a drink from the wooden bucket, it was called the *cuinneag*, which would be standing beside the door, with a lid on it. But the men said, "This water has been in the *cuinneag* all night, we want it fresh from the well." So she went to get it, and when she came back the roof was afire. She was in a terrible state, "What will I do? what will I do?" And they said, "Do what the crows do."'

The historian Eric Richards has written recently that the Clearances have 'receded into the distant past' and well beyond personal memory.[3] It does not feel like that in Sleat. Mary Morrison, who died quite recently, told me how she heard about the clearance of Boreraig from her father, who was a boy at the time and was related to the widow Flora Matheson: 'One thing that he always used to mention, he remembered the bailiffs putting out the fire with the basins of milk—you know that they set the milk for cream to make butter, and they put out the fires with the basins of milk, and I suppose a small boy would remember that, because in those days milk was very precious at that time...' Likewise Neil MacRae, a boy aged seven who famously defied the estate heavies, saying 'If my father was here today, who would dare do this to us!'—Neil is still remembered with pride by his family in Strathpeffer. Alex MacRae showed me a photo of Neil, his grandfather, taken in a hayfield in the 1920s. And Peggy MacKinnon of Heast, granddaughter of Farquhar Kelly, one of the twins, knew that the man of the family had been 'away in Loundy [the Lowlands], taking in the harvest with his own sickle' and that the family carried away with them, along with the gear and bedding, some stones from their houses, presumably the valuable lintels, and even the potatoes they had already planted.

Some lintels in Boreraig are still in place over the doorways and window spaces. The houses are handsome, unusually tall with doors that don't make you stoop. The walls are so well masoned that massive stones fit perfectly with a minimum of rubble to wedge them, and some have binks or cupboard spaces neatly built in. The townland is sheltered from the ocean by Beinn Buidhe to the west, looking south across Loch Eishort with its islands and skerries, and its waters teeming with crab and lobster. In the autumn stags bawl and girn from the coastal slopes across the loch, between Ord and Morsaig (from which Alastair MacKinnon's second-cousin's family were evicted). The whole place still flickers with life—non-human life, that is. Unusually dark wrens of the Hebridean sub-species have made the houses their own. When David Paterson was there in 1999, he found a golden eagle dead inside one of

the house shells and heard a whoosh as its mate flew low overhead. Curlews pipe and probe along the shore. Ash trees line the burn, which is bridged by a long plank of sedimentary rock, and the gullies above the village are full of hazels, which will have offered a high-calorie harvest in the autumn.

The goodness and civilisation of the place reach back into history and prehistory. A sacred stone stands tall at the head of the fields, near a boundary dyke still used as a seamark by the Heast fishermen when they have to avoid a dangerous reef called the Bogha Mor, 'the great bulge'. These fields are so level that there was no need to build

lazybeds, since the earth could be turned with the *cas chrom*, the foot plough. The remnant of a dun stands on a craggy headland at the western entrance to the township. So the past of Boreraig can still be touched, and heard. Farquhar Kelly survived to give evidence to the Deer Forest Commission in 1892 and was the last person to be buried over the hill at Cill Chriosd in Strath Suardal. He would have been carried out from Heast past Cnoc na Tuireadh, 'hill of the wailing', along a path that the Boreraig people had laboured to make into a track. They culverted and bridged and broke stones for hard-core. By the time of the clearance they had reached north from the clachan to the watershed, where mail was left for them at an upright stone. (Perhaps it is still the same stone that is standing on the verge, near a new gate). As Neil MacKinnon said to us, 'Their road is beautifully made. It is enough to bring tears to your eyes, that they did not remain to get the good of it.'

House below Beinn Bhuidhe, Boreraig

Detail of stone-work and lintel at Boreraig

Post-Clearance house at Boreraig, with Loch Eishort

Eas na Muc—The Falls of the Pig, Boreraig

The north shore of Loch Eishort, looking towards Boreraig

Seagrass and machair near Scarasta, Harris

Lazybeds at Mealista, Lewis

STIOMRABHAIGH, LEWIS – OUTER HEBRIDES

When you enter Stiomrabhaigh on the north shore of Loch Sealg, greenness rises round you, acres of still-sweet grass draped in a mantle over the shoulder-bones and flanks of rocky outcrops. The *lodan* or tidal lochan drains in a rippling brown current you can jump across at low tide, into the *tob* or bay that slants south-east towards the Sound of Shiant. On the true-left bank of the channel a stand of aspens chatters its leafage like hail pattering across a roof.

On slopes and in little dales where sheep now graze, the turf is shaped all over by the works that the people of this township laboured to make. Lazybeds stripe the shallow slopes. On the marshy area up above, a field of bog cotton has invaded the moss where peats used to be dug. An outcrop has been sheared, planed and split into right-angled corners for stone to make the settlement. At its heart is a network of walls, houses, barns, byres, kilns and dykes. Two of these houses have 12-ft gables and sharp corners—evidently more recent homes. The more elaborate, uphill from the shore, has a D-shaped field on its south-east corner, presumably a kailyard. The other is protected by a terrace of stones against encroaching marshiness. Even the ring-dyke round the townland is more stone than turf.

No civilisation here now. A heron skreighs and is joined by another, giving rise to a rare double skreigh. The fish they catch will once have been corralled in the fish-trap whose twin walls meet in a funnel shape in the *lodan*. Stiomrabhaigh (Stemreway in the older spelling) stood out against clearance for decades after its fellow townships (nine of them round the shores of Loch Sealg and lower Loch Seaforth) had been emptied 'like sheep driven by dogs into a fank and their fires drowned on the hearths by the officers of the estate', as John Smith remembered his eviction from Eishken, two miles up the loch from Stiomrabhaigh in the 1830s.[1] Here a sporting estate was created, complete with a fleet of anglers' boats headed by a steam yacht called the *Puffin*. The place is still in fine order, full of persons with fishing-rods and Barbour jackets and keepers in well-tailored green tweeds—owned by a nightclub and arcade proprietor from Lancashire who has recently tried to privatise the public road into Eishken from the north.

The people of Stiomrabhaigh could hold on for a time because they had been canny enough to sign long leases. 'Over the years, they had been harassed by Estate officials and farm employees alike including the usual allegation of sheep stealing.'[2] As Dan MacLeod of Lemreway put it to me, 'They were a thorn in the flesh of the estate.' At last, in 1858, the twenty families, numbering eighty people, Nicolsons and MacMillans, MacInneses and Fergusons, flitted to Lemreway, to Grabhir, and to the more exposed coast to the north. On their trek out of the townships the Lewis folk used to carry their children and their gear on their backs and drive their stock in front of them. Sometimes the men had to float their roof timbers across an arm of a loch or a sea-loch and sleep under upturned boats while they built huts out of turf.[3] As so often, the veritable experience of such events is still alive in people's memories. On the Atlantic coast of the island, a chief Napier witness, Norman Morrison from Brenish—which is now the last inhabited township on the coastal road south from Uig—recalled the days in the 1830s when people cleared from Mealista, the next township south, were 'thrown in amongst us' by the estate management, giving rise to unbearable congestion: 'The rest were hounded away to Australia and America, and I think I hear the cry of the children till this day.'[4] When I mentioned his evidence to people in Uig, they said, 'Oh yes, Tormod Ruadh—he was red-haired like all the Morrisons.'

Some miles to the north-east, tourists who flock to marvel at the towering elegance of the stone circle at Callanish or the massive complex broch at Carloway should know that in 1851 the crofters there, who had been living on shellfish while they built new houses to the specification of the estate, were summarily evicted after 'a very, very bad year... and some of the houses are half-built and the people in Canada'.[5] Of course the livelihood had become for a time almost impossible. In spite of this, according to the lists of the Chamberlain of the Lews who managed the huge estate for Sir James Matheson, in township after township the proportion of families who declared themselves willing to emigrate was rarely more than a small minority.[6]

A generation later one of this manager's successors tried to counter a demand for Stiomrabhaigh to be returned to its people by arguing that it was too far from the good fishing grounds off the Shiant Islands. Refuting this, the fishermen of Crossbost pointed out that 'There was no more suitable or convenient place on the coast to fish [the Shiant banks] than Orinsay and a successful fishing industry had existed before the evictions'.[7] Orinsay (now spelt Orosay) is a mere mile by sea from Stiomrabhaigh, whose people knew the Shiants intimately. One of them, Neil Nicolson, was the chief source of Shiant place-names when the government surveyors came here a few years before the flitting.[8]

In 1891 the men of the South Lochs 'encamped on prime grazing ground about a hundred yards from the foreshore at Orinsay and Stemreway' and 'worked hard at establishing a camp'. When a farmer came to warn them out, 'a portion of the land had been dug'. Arrested and charged, they were defended by Donald MacRae—a leader some years earlier of a joyous deer-forest raid a few miles south. (This is celebrated by Will MacLean and Jim Crawford's massive windowed cairn at the junction of the A859 and the B8060.) Having duly been convicted, they were marched in handcuffs to do fourteen days in prison at Inverness. After another thirty years of the Crofters' War—interrupted by the Great War, which steeled the spirit of those who survived—the families reoccupied Orosay and Stiomrabhaigh. They rebuilt the walls of the houses and 'cov-

ered them all over with a thatch of heather. That's what everyone did, built a black house with the material they could get and they were quite happy with that and good land and good fishing to go along with it', according to the son of one of the men.[9]

Orosay now has a few good houses and a road. Two families clung on in Stiomrabhaigh, which is reached only by a path, till 1944, when old age and the War forced them out. The cairn on a green knoll at the seaward end of the clachan was built when Pairc Historical Society visited in 1991, and there is a Bible inside it. You could see it as a memorial especially commemorating the two young Calbost men from five land-raiding families who were ferrying in building materials in 1926 and were 'drowned at the entrance of Loch Shell in sight of the land they promised themselves'.[10]

Tob Stiomrabhaigh—Stemreway Cove

Keep, or store, at Stiomrabhaigh

Tigh nan Cailleachan Dubha—The Nuns' House—Mealista

Evening at Mol Foirs Geodha, Mealista

Burial ground at Bhaile na Cille, Uig Bay

Scarasta, Harris

Donald MacDonald lives at Horgabost in south-west Harris, at the mouth of a little glen that opens out onto machair meadows fringed by the immaculate pale-gold beaches of that coast. He sings the *Oran nan Fuadaichean* – 'Song of the Clearances' (here translated by his daughter Joina) in a steady tenor without much ornament:

Listen to me, people of the hills,
Pay attention, lads.
Everyone who hears this song,
Join in tunefully.

Our relatives were evicted,
Some to the cold misty hills
And to America overseas –
That's how we heard the stories.

Soldiers came from the Queen
Wrongfully to this place
And cleared the best side of it –
The rest went to the Bays.

They put sheep in their place,
Cheviots and the antlered deer.
When the struggle with tyranny began,
None of them were injured...

Loch Broom* is doing his utmost
To defame us
Because we ploughed the plots
Which our forebears rightfully owned.

Gaels were in the green hills
Where there are springs to drink from.
Now the place where people earned their living
Is overgrown with thistles.

Grandfathers were in the place
And grandmothers of the kindly heroes.
There was no lack of good upbringing,
Butter and warm milk and meat.

If my kinsfolk will listen to me,
I will ask of them the right
To elect McDermid†
To the Western Isles of the mist.

*Roderick MacLeay, owner of Scaristaveg, from which the songwriter's great-grandfather was evicted in the 1830s.
†John MacKinnon MacDermid of Mull, Labour candidate (and runner-up) for the Western Isles in the 1929 General Election.

This song was written by Neil MacDonald of Luskentyre, on the other side of the bay. He called it *Oran na Raididh* – 'Song of the Land Raids'. For his part in reclaiming the land of his forebears at the south end of the machair he served a total of six months in prison.

Memories of the clearance have survived. Soldiers of the 78th Regiment were brought in from Fort George at the bidding of Lord Dunmore (who had bought Harris for £60,000 in 1834 and sold half of it at 250 per cent profit thirty years later). To enforce the removals, Donald MacDonald told me, 'full pails of milk were poured away on a stone beside a house'. This was Norman MacKenzie's house. The stone became the cornerstone of a new house built recently by his great-grandson.[1] Roofs were burnt, and some people were allowed to carry away their roof-timbers to their new places on the east coast. Donald was told this by his father, who had it from a Drinishader man evicted from Seilebost as a boy. Kirsty Shaw of Tarbert told me some years ago how her great-grandmother, a crofter at Crago, two miles east of Horgabost, had her house 'burnt to a cinder when the men came to put them out. She had to hide among the corn, in one of the furrows... with her daughter in her arms.'

No corn there now, or anywhere in Harris. The *feannagan* on which it grew stripe the slopes above the western machair in an immense corduroy or tweed, which stretches from the verge of the shell-sand meadows to the skyline at three hundred feet above sea-level. The weaving of it came to an abrupt end when Dunmore and his factor Donald Stewart brought in their new regime. 'Are you pleased now I've burnt the houses?' Stewart asked his wife. 'I'll never be pleased while I see a wisp of smoke between here and Rodel.' And so 'their fires were quenched by order of the estate.'[2] Stewart built his own base on Ensay, the low-lying island which is the eastern end of the land bridge from Harris to North Uist via Killigray, Pabbay and Berneray. These islands were full of oats and barley grown by crofters until they were completely cleared. The lazybeds still stripe Ensay in exquisite patterns like watered silk. They cover every square yard of the land from the central watershed down to the little cliffs of the western shore. If you think of the work that went into them to make the people's staple food and drink—the many stills on Pabbay were a fine excuse for clearing it—they are the people's handprints and fingerprints, and they are indelible. Their perfect herring-boning and dovetailing must have been achieved by precise cooperation

between many families over generations, and by grievous labour. Bones of Ensay women dug up recently on the island show that they suffered early in life from osteoarthritis of the spine. Nowadays the place is nothing but a wild garden. The gutters are a darker green of broad-bladed grass starred with buttercups and a few tormentils. The ridges are paler green with short grass and the honey-blond seed-heads of bentgrass, gemmed with the purples, yellows and whites of bugloss, tormentil and eyebright.

There is an almost total dearth of houses from Luskentyre to Scarastaveg and from Ensay across to eastern Berneray. On Ensay the stones of the homesteads have been re-used in the long dykes that run straight from the back of Stewart's old mansion westward to the skyline. These are the fields in which he pastured his prize bulls and experimented with some of the first horse-drawn seeders in the Highlands. The big house—now owned by 'a man from London'—is fading into dereliction. Its slates are sliding off, water stains the panelling in the lounge, and white sand is drifting up the steps that lead from the terrace to the shore.

At least a few stones were kept by the crofters. The forebears of Norman MacLeod of Bridge House, Obbe (Leverburgh), lived on Pabbay, Ensay and St Kilda. When the Ensay folk were cleared, they carried with them the invaluable door and window lintels, made of hard grey stone. They are now steps to the upper level of Norman's garden. (Killigray had been a good source of stone which split evenly). He showed me a massive tablet amongst the seaweed nearby at Carminish which had been meant for a tombstone. It came to grief while it was being shipped into the natural harbour where the Earl of Dunmore used to land from his steam yacht before being driven in a horse-drawn carriage to his first headquarters down at Rodel.

The civilisation of Ensay had been long-lived and deep-rooted. A standing stone raises a finger at the high point of the eastern ridge—one of a local group set up for half-sacred, half-astronomical purposes in pre-Christian times. Sand-blow has recently laid bare a chapel at the north end with low walls built of barely-masoned stones. It was probably on a site first colonised by some of Columba's people in the 7th century. At the back of the big house a group of colossal whale ribs and a vertebra remind us that the seas as well as the croftlands were ravaged in the furious industrial activity of the mid 19th century.

The crofters were banished to Nova Scotia, especially to Cape Breton Island, and to the Bays of eastern Harris. It is the latter which is remembered today as a kind of doom and was felt to be so at the time, 'so surrounded by rocks that sometimes we never see the sun at all', as Roderick Ross of Geocrab told the Napier Commissioners in 1883.[3] The Bays are like a storm sea frozen; the houses are like small boats locked in its troughs; but at least the island of Scalpay was well placed for fishing. The Pabbay people were sent there en masse. Norman MacLeod suggests that it was this cohesion which kept them bound together as a community. Today they have a new bridge to Harris and a new seafood factory which employs twenty-eight people.*

There was little room in the Bays for *feannagan* much longer than an average flowerbed, and no room at all for the dead. The west-side burial grounds at Scarasta and Borve, and especially at Luskentyre, testify to the hundreds of journeys made with coffins through the mountains from Geocrab and Finsbay, Scalpay and Flodabay, Drinishader and Plocrapool, Scadabay and Cuidnish. Poor roads were a grievance with many Napier witnesses in Harris, most strikingly a Plocrapool fisherman called Angus Campbell. He wanted a bridge over the Lusken river (now called the Laxdale), 'for I have seen the coffins upon our shoulders dragged through the flood—six men strung together and following the course of the stream to keep themselves from being swept away with the bier upon their shoulders'.[4] Today the parapets of the first bridge still stand on either bank, while just downstream the three big concrete tunnels of the latest bridge show how big a torrent is liable to flood down the channel.

All this is a far cry from the more comfortable life of the western islands, evoked in a song translated for me by Neil Campbell of Scalpay, whose mother's people came from Pabbay:

It was not the peat or the bogs of Scalpay
That I was used to
But the fine machair lands of Pabbay.

It was not the poor bothy with sods for a back wall
That I had in my country,
In the beautiful sandy island.

The lovely green-coloured island is beautiful with flowers.
If I had my wish I would be there alive
And would be buried there.

*This plant is Norwegian-owned. It opened at a cost of £3.8 million in 2001.

The island of Sromay, with Ensay (left) and Pabbay on the horizon

East Harris, near Geocrab

Burial-ground at Luskentyre

House at Rubha na Moine, with West Loch Tarbert & Beinn Dhubh

Thatched house at Port Ludaig, Berneray

North Uist and its satellite islands to north and east, which count as part of Harris, are as much water as land. Walking or driving over them, sailing past or between them, you can feel on your skin the effort it has taken to extract a living from them. The likes of Sursay and Tahay, Hermetray and Vaccasay, now look good for little. As we are told by one of the most eloquent of all the Napier witnesses, Malcolm MacLeod, a cottar chosen to speak for Berneray, Sursay was 'a good island…for peats and pasture' and Hermetray too was offshore pasture for the Berneray crofters.[1] When the price of kelp dropped in the 1820s, the wage for cutting it was itself cut, and the industry fell away to almost nothing. The crofters' income shrank and they could not pay their rents. Lord Dunmore's factor, MacDonald, seized their stock in lieu and also took over the islets for his own herds and flocks.

That scraps of land which barely rise clear of the sea should be crucial to livelihood points to the difficulties of living in such a place. They were not all natural. MacLeod testified that when the people began to fish for lobsters after losing their cattle pastures, 'the factor MacDonald sent the ground officer to stop us, he being angry because we were not going to Australia.' This remembered history felt very close as I walked all over the downlands of Berneray and their living embroidery of flowers with a lobster fisherman called Angus MacLeod. He talked almost continuously, in the teeth of a blasting gale which had kept his boat tied up. In story after story he laid bare what it had been like to live here before and after clearance cut its swathe. Stories of the big farmer's herdsman impounding stray animals whenever his wife told him that she was 'without tea'. Stories of women working 'like horses, bringing the seaweed up there on their backs' to create potato land high up on the slopes of Moor Hill and Sand Hill after the much easier and more fertile ground to the south had been taken over by the new big farm at Borve.

These islands north of Uist, all green today, will have been blond once with the oats they ground and ate and the barley they parched, then cooked in the *poit dubh* for the distilling of whisky. Stories of cheating and outfacing the gaugers (the excisemen) abound.[2] Pabbay was the granary of Harris. Twenty-six families lived there before the clearance. Fifteen years ago a man from Perthshire knew a woman who had met a Pabbay refugee, Rachel Mhor. She had been born in the open, as snow drifted, after the evicting officer hauled her mother out of the house on a blanket and nailed up the door. The family fled across the Sound to Harris and survived as squatters on the machair meadow.

From Boreray, the most westerly of the small islands, you could swim to the low-lying coast of Uist, to the shore of the long shell-sand neb called Machair Leathann which runs north from Sollas. Where the wild ground gives way to croftland, the turf littered with stones is a battlefield, although there is no crossed-swords symbol on the map. The stone-heaps are the ruins of a siege carried out on the crofters' homes by Lord MacDonald of Clanranald's 'army' and the Sheriff's constables. The estate was desperate to clear debts of a quarter of a million pounds. Only lets to sheep-farmers from the mainland would balance the books. In early August 1849 the Sollas women fought with shingle stones and stems of tangle to save their homes from being torched and dismantled. Finally they were left to bathe their split scalps with water from the burn after the truncheons had done their work.[3] The little burn, which runs into the sea at Ard a Phuind, is called Abhainn na Fala, 'river of blood', as I was told by Archie Morrison who lived nearby at Struan.

This clearance is known as *Blar Sholais*, the Battle of Sollas. It was fought over several days. Like the other clearances towards the end of the whole process (Knoydart, Strath Carron), it was especially brutal. At the end of it 117 families had been evicted for arrears of rent.[4] As was often the case, it was mainly the women who fought the law-men and the estate heavies. Maybe this was because the men, as the formal tenants, were chary of doing anything illegal. After the Battle it was four men who were taken away in handcuffs and sentenced

Detail of house at Locheport, North Uist

to four months in prison for rioting and obstructing the police. Before their trial in Lochmaddy they were held in cells behind what is now the Old Courthouse. It is now a very pleasant Bed & Breakfast establishment and as you eat your meal you look out on a walled garden which used to be the prison yard. The householder, Norman Johnston, quarry worker and county councillor, had heard from a Sollas man 'that his father always hated the sight of this place, because he remembered the noise, the thud-thud-thud of the hammers the prisoners used to soften the fibres of the oakum.' Crofters who remained in Sollas and some who were scattered to other parts can tell us from their grandparents' stories how the people were forced out. Murdo McCuish of Middlequarter told me his story as we stood at the side of the track running north beside the pale-gold crescent of Traigh Iar. This is a flawless Hebridean beach whose beauty was a liability to the crofters because the soft sand made the horses struggle as they carted seaweed from the nearest reefs. Murdo had heard from his grandmother (died 1929: aged eleven in 1849) how her family 'knew they wouldn't have much time to get the loom out, so they were just going to leave the loom in and cut the tweed out of the loom. But the next thing they knew, they had fired the thatch, and it was so dry the sparks were coming in through the thatch, and they had to evacuate the house. The loom and the tweed were burnt in the house.' The Sheriff-Substitute for the Outer Hebrides later ridiculed the notion that the evictions had been 'merciless'.[5]

The shattering of the community was so sudden that even the memory of it was splintered. Thirty-four Sollas families were relocated to the boggy shore of Loch Eport nine miles to the south-east, with the generous permission of the landlord and the expert advice of a Free Church minister. Here they had to build themselves 'clod shacks' on ground so soft that the children's feet sank in when they played. Peggy Morrison, who lived there, told me that her grandfather, one of the four imprisoned men, 'could not bear to see the burning of the houses', and that when forced emigrants were being embarked for Glasgow and Australia, 'they were taking the women by their long hair and swinging them in. It was like Africa.' Although she knew that a tweed had been burnt in a loom, she did not know whose it was until I told her.

The resistance of the Sollas people was fierce and it was bound to fail. Here were families so depleted by the Potato Famine and further gravelled by near slavery on what is still called the Committee Road, a pointless track from Sollas across the hill to Claddach-kyles on the Atlantic coast. The wage for working on it was three-halfpence for an 8-hour day (one penny for a woman)—which they had already earned in oatmeal at 1lb per head per day. The strongest man in Sollas was Alasdair Mor, Big Alasdair Matheson. On the eve of the evictions he walked five miles east to Dusary for a sack of meal to feed his family. The heavies, afraid of his strength, had waited for this moment to drive the people out. Big Alasdair came home to find his house in ruins. He had been the only person strong enough to lift a certain hefty angular boulder. It is still there amongst the heather between the road and the shore, near Botarua at the south end of Vallay strand, marked with red paint 'because we think these things should be remembered.'[6]

Boat at Loch nan Geirann, North Uist

Former croft-house at Sollas

Turf-covered house at Loch a' Bhaigh, Berneray

The fertile west side of Berneray, with Pabbay on the horizon

Barn at South Glendale, South Uist

In South Uist, when they talk about 'the back of the hill' they mean the east side, the region between the sea and the two 2,000-foot mountains, Hecla and Beinn Mhor. People settled here over the generations and built up small clachans where the burns pouring down from the hills had made spreads of arable soil. According to Donald MacLean of Howmore, lobster fisherman and lighthouse boatman, it had been a better place to make a living than the western machairs because those grasslands based on blown sand were so friable that even the planting of potatoes could destabilise them: 'The glens round at the back of the hill were good for cattle, the Minch was fish-rich.' He had found deep holes in the rocks where limpets were pounded to make ground-bait and shingle stones well above the shoreline where fish were spread to cure.

By 1841 when the first Census was taken, 168 people had been evicted from the coast between Loch Skiport and Loch Eynort, from the clachans of Corrodale and Hellisdale, Usinish and Lamasay. To make room for sheep-farms they were removed to break in barren land, 'black moor', round Loch Boisdale at the south end of the island, or accept small crofts on rocky Eriskay, or emigrate to Canada.

At Mol a Dheas (shingle-beach of the south) in the bight of the Usinish peninsula, shells of houses with rounded corners stand above the high-tide-mark. In one of them lived Catherine MacAulay . She was a well-spring of the luxuriant pre-Reformation poetry, such as the wondrously tender *Oran nan Buadh*, the 'Invocation of the Graces'. Evicted and therefore homeless and destitute, 'She wandered about from house to house, and from townland to townland, warmly welcomed and cordially received wherever she went.' Duncan MacLellan, a crofter at Carnan ten miles north of Mol a Dheas, remembered thirty years later 'the people who crowded his father's house to hear her night after night, and week after week... The discussions that followed her recitations were realistic and instructive.' The poem begins by calling down good qualities on a young woman about to be married:

> I bathe your palms
> In showers of wine,
> In purifying fire,
> In the seven elements,
> In the juice of raspberries,
> In the milky honey...

It foreshadows a hard life for people who leave the island:

> The town there is dark
> And dark the people in it.
> You are the brown swan
> Going in among them...[1]

The powers invoked are Celtic as well as Christian, Eimhir and Maebh as well as Mary and Jesus. The poem was so potent that when Alexander Carmichael the exciseman was on his way home to Benbecula, wading waist-deep across the South Ford after taking the words down from the Carnan crofter, 'all he was conscious of was the roll and the singing of the waters, and the rhythm' of Catherine's 'Invocation'.[2]

Such was the culture which was being scattered and injured by the emptying of the eastern coast. The experience of being cleared was described by Donald MacLellan, a crofter from Garrynamonie in the south-west lowland of the island. His father's family were evicted from Corrodale, a few miles south of Catherine MacAulay's place. 'We then went away with boats to a place twelve miles from the first, where there was no people, no houses, but heavy heather; sleeping in shore dens, with frost and snow covering our beds for five days and five nights, until they made turf cottages. We then made better houses in summer...'[3] This was at Hartabhaigh, south of Loch Boisdale, from which they were removed to Eriskay, and from which they were moved north again to the shores of Loch Eynort, where they lived as cottars on the big farm of Bornish.

The petty oppression which people endured there can be learned from Donald's great-grandson Angus, who in the 1960s became the island's chief recorded storyteller and memorialist or *seannachd*. In place of the cattle they had pastured on the hill they were allowed one cow, and they had to struggle in the law court at Lochmaddy against the island's new owner Lady Cathcart (whose father had ordered the original clearance) for the right to keep a dog. They won, provided each dog had a collar. They were forced to take their corn to the owner's mill for grinding, and the ground officers (known as *abaghan*, terriers) 'began to go through the houses breaking the querns [handmills], and the querns were thrown out into a loch down at Ormaclate beside the main road'– known since then as Loch nam Braithnean, 'the loch of the querns'.[4]

Rising population and the capitalisation of agriculture herded the people into the west and south of the island, giving rise to the extraordinary settlement pattern today. Dozens of houses scatter like children's bricks on a carpet over the flat lands from Kildonan south by Daliburgh and Kilpheder to Garynamonie. Each is widely separated from its neighbour, yet there are so many that from several vantage-points they as look as continuous as a street.

Very few are on a meaningful site, in terms of water supply, shelter, proximity to a river, a loch, a meeting-place, a junction, or anything at all. On the rim of the country with the Atlantic pounding and roaring a few yards away, these dwellings are scarcely more ensconced than igloos in the Arctic. All over the Highlands the people had lamented their dispersal from clachans into crofts. 'I have seen a woman weeping at being separated from her neighbours,' Donald Morrison of Geocrab in Harris told the Napier Commissioners in 1883.[5] 'When the crofts were made the women didn't like it,' John MacAulay of Illeray, Baleshare, North Uist, told me in 1988, 'because [formerly] if something went wrong, they had only had to go around the corner.' A grid was imposed by the owners, through their surveyors and factors, with little regard for natural habits or social wellbeing.

As land hunger bit deep in the later 19th century, South Uist people fought for a better livelihood. They set up road blocks and cut telephone wires, to make the government pay attention. They raided disused land, as Donald MacLellan did on the islet of Calvay at the head of Loch Eynort. He took off eighty bags of potatoes in a year, with the help of little Angus who filled creels with seaweed to fertilise the ground: 'The people were doing the place good, breaking in the land, land that was going wild, that wasn't producing grass or crops until it was manured.'[6]

Loch Eynort had been the marrow of the island. In the 16th century there was even a nunnery on its sinuous and sheltered north shore, at Arinambane. It is commemorated in a perfect quatrain collected by Carmichael in the 1880s:

A lovely summer shieling of one tree,
Behind the wind, in front of the sun,
Where we could see the whole of the world
And no man could us see.

Remnants of its fabric still show in the ground– the wide arc of the ring-dyke, the stripes of lazybeds, the parallel boulders of a boat-landing running into the sea and the taller walls of a later inn that ended its days as the home of the one person left there by 1881, an incoming shepherd.[7] On the level ground opposite Calvay there stands a stone shell with rounded corners and a chimney stack. This was Tigh a' Mhail, the rent house. Here people came to pay their dues in kind. Their ingrained resentment at exaction and subordination lives on in Angus MacLellan's terrific story about a tenant who was faulted for bringing just too little corn for his rent: 'What did Gille Padra' Dubh do but catch hold of the factor and stick his knife in the factor's throat and hold him above the peck measure until he had filled it with his blood. "It'll be full now," he said. That's as true as can be. That was the last rent ever collected there!' So life was lived round the long harbour of Loch Eynort, the living hard-won and shot through with fantasies of revenge and lucky escape.

'The back of the hill' – houses on the north shore of Loch Skiport, beneath Hecla

The present-day community at Kilpheder

Hartabhaigh, with Skye on the eastern horizon

The shallows between Benbecula and South Uist

Three generations of houses at South Boisdale, South Uist

The Sound of Fuday at Eoligarry

The grimly handsome house beside the main road at Greian in north Barra, with its pair of wings, its Georgian windows and derelict kitchen-garden sheltered by high walls from the Atlantic winds, dominates the neighbourhood with an unmistakable air of command. Who can have lived here? The factor perhaps, or some other overseer who saw to the clearing of the island? It was both, in the person of the Reverend Henry Beatson, the Church of Scotland minister who came to Barra from Greenock via Skye in 1847, just in time to hound people starving and destitute after the Potato Famine onto the quays and into the holds of the emigrant ships in Castlebay harbour.[1] He was a Presbyterian Protestant on a Roman Catholic island and he married the daughter of Colonel MacNeill's factor. No wonder his house looks like some sort of head-quarters. It stands above the townland which slopes in a shallow green howe towards the gleaming links of the river. Also in view is the new Catholic graveyard with its nakedly emotional epitaphs. One granite stone is for Morag MacAulay, Mor Bhan, died in February 1998 aged 86: 'Fuilt Bhan–Sorely Missed'. In 1988 she sang for me, in her best dress with her hair newly curled, a song which a Uist man had written in her praise between the two World Wars. Gaelic, the first language of the island, would have been foreign to Beatson. From the stronghold of his manse he deplored the badly behaved natives who broke into food-stores when they were starving and pretended to be even poorer than they were to qualify for handouts of meal–administered by his wife.[2] Greian is still steeped in the peculiar emptiness that prevails after the *fear thollaidh nan tighean*, the destroyer of homes, has gutted a settlement. Roderick MacNeill, known as Rory Rum the Storyman, was the best climber, fowler and storyteller on Mingulay in the middle of the 19th century. He had been evicted from Greian in 1825: 'My fresh new house was burned over my head, and I burned my hands rescuing my dear little children. The terrible time that was. The land was taken from us, though we were not a penny in debt, and all the lands of the townland were given to a lowland farmer beside us.'[3]

Once the hereditary owners, the MacNeills, had sold the island to Colonel Gordon, an exceedingly rich man from Aberdeenshire, the clearance became ever more drastic. People were moved wholesale from the ample lands of the north to the steep and rocky south-east. Niall MacPherson of Buaile nam Bodach calls his township 'a transit camp for the dispossessed'. The cottages that housed them were built perforce in marshy hollows near the shore where typhoid flourished. One of them is known as the Plague House. Here an old man and his daughter survived on mussels left outside by their frightened neighbours until he died and she lifted him with difficulty into a coffin which was then hauled out by a rope thrown through the door. The dead man's great-granddaughter, Mairi Jane MacLean, lives some miles north at Eoligarry, which was bought by the government for the good of the crofters in 1901. Her stories make an epic of the evictions–and the reclamations. She thinks of the Revd Henry Beatson as 'synonymous with heartlessness' and tells the story of a man cleared from Greian down to Borve, 'dying at one end of a house, he wouldn't last many more days, and his daughter was giving birth at the other, death and life at either end, and neither had any place in the inhumanity.'

Borve on the west coast is remarkable in the Hebrides for its fairly roomy fields with dry-stone dykes that make a grey-checked pattern on the green of the now fallow arable. Clearly it was once a good working settlement. If you go to the end of its northern road and walk up the hill, you come upon the poor remains of the houses where people cleared from elsewhere had to perch on ground unfit for habitation. Borve's representative at the Napier hearing in Castlebay was a crofter called Michael Buchanan, a famous speaker on land-rights in the churchyard after Sunday worship. His weekly talks were 'awaited with the same eagerness' as radio bulletins in the wars to come.[4] He testified that nineteen families had been forced onto Borve, fourteen of them from Greian and Cliad, and that 'I have seen with my own eyes the roof of the house actually falling down upon the fire, and smoke issuing' when 'the houses were knocked down' after an eviction.[5] Cliad, on the coast north of Greian, lives again because it was reclaimed by the crofters in 1900. Now it is full of decent new houses, old ones turned into sheds or garages, newish off-road vehicles and cars, and gardens dug into lazybeds for potatoes. Mairi Jane MacLean was told by her father, who was seven at the time, how men whose fathers had been forced down to Borve came into Cliad to get their lands back. They harnessed two horses, one black and one white, to a metal plough.

This was '*the* acquisition above all. And he never forgot how the horses' manes rippled on their heads as they worked; they were going up and down, up and down.' The men gathered 'where they could be seen, down by the shore. The women and children were all standing round; they made it a kind of holiday, and maybe it coincided with a Holiday of Obligation. The grieve [farm manager]—he would be a non-Catholic—he said, "You're on MacGillivray's land!" And the men said, "We are going to make our mark." Every man put his hand to the plough, to show their solidarity. They would be ploughing two or three strips each. It was only a token, there was no violence. "Jonathan," they said, "where do you want?" He was my uncle, and he was very quiet: "Here will do." And that was the croft he later got, No. 7. They threw up little shacks here and there. My father's sister was the first child born in Cliad since the clearance—her mother had been unwell so she had never gone to Canada. Yes, that was the way of it, and my father said he would never forget them, the two horses, black and white, and their manes going up and down.'

Cattle at Eoligarry, with South Uist and Fuday behind

The hearth of the 'plague house' at Buaile nam Bodach

The beach at Bagh Siar, Vatersay

Vatersay, immediately south of Barra, is shaped like a Chinese ideogram or a bone from some unknown mammal. Its slender neck, flanked by blond beaches, expands again southward into a little world of the purest green pastures in the Hebrides, which give good feeding to more than a hundred cattle. This rare physical goodness was the scene of struggle after struggle as the Crofters' War entered its second and final phase.

In September 1900, not long after the symbolic ploughing and reclaiming of Cliad in north Barra, landless men from the south of that island landed on Vatersay and pegged out crofts for themselves. What they desired was 'a piece of land to plant a barrel or two of potatoes and grazing for a cow, to fall back on when the fishing failed'. They maintained this beachhead for years, empowered by knowing that 'their grandparents and remoter ancestors had crofts. . .at the very place where the raiders' huts were now set up–and though their grandparents had been evicted their descendants had never given up their claim'. Throughout all the years since, their descendants down to this day have continued to bury their dead on Vatersay.'[1]

The spirit of these raiders, or settlers, sings in *Hu a ho gum b'eibhinn leam*, written by Michael Buchanan, the spokesman for Borve in Barra, who was 'a good scholar, and a bard into the bargain'.

The refrain goes:

> *What happy news for me*
> *To hear how you got on*
> *And how you told them plainly in Edinburgh*
> *That your camp would not retreat.*

At least fifty cottars from Barra landed on Vatersay. By 1907 twenty houses had been built–and ten men imprisoned for two months. In 1908 the Congested Districts Board bought the island from Lady Cathcart and all the settlers were granted crofts. Buchanan's song bears witness to the turbulent stir of ideas in the community:

> *Eogan there in Eorasdal,*
> *See what a Tory he is*
> *And if he won't follow Donald's orders* *
> *We'll just vote him down to the Glen.*[†]

Other verses rejoice in their natural resources:

> *You have seaweed rights from the North Beach*
> *Out to Snuasimul harbour*
> *And Uinessan along with it,*
> *And Nor nan Ceann's grave is there.*
>
> *You have the Caolas, good arable;*
> *You have drift seaweed at Port a' Bhata,*
> *And you can dry the grain there*
> *In the kiln that Melvin had.*[2]

You can feel the people's deep attachment to the place in the naming of each landmark. The reborn Eorasdal or Eorisdale was a row of cottages with free-standing 'steamies' or wash-houses near the shoreline of the south-eastern bay. They were built with government help in what turned out to be a brief renaissance of crofting before the First World War. The houses are empty now and black and brown cattle graze between stone gables like big gravestones. They had been roomy, compared with the old black-houses, and they had been fairly cheap, with walls of crinkly tin whose remaining sheets shiver in the wind and whose thin floorboards now lie in heaps of matchwood. Their masonry is much poorer than that of the large farmer's house which stands isolated to the west of the modern village, like a memorial to Vatersay's era as a sheep-ranch.

In the 1990s a causeway was finally built, joining Vatersay to Barra as Eriskay is now joined to South Uist, Berneray to North Uist, and Scalpay to Harris. So life is easier for the dourly self-contained people of the island. Instead of buffeting across the channel in the small open ferryboat which people used to share with a collie dog and a sack of onions, the islanders can nip up to Castlebay in their own cars and the nurse or doctor can come to them. The many cattle give the green lands the look of an earlier Highland epoch, as do the numerous ploughed fields on the sandy slopes above the graveyard, beyond the huddle of newly-built brown and white houses.

*Domhall Mhicheil, the raiders' leader, known as 'The Government'.

†The congested settlement for cleared and landless people just east of Castlebay.

The 'big house' and village of Vatersay

The shells of houses at Eorisdale

Eorisdale

REFERENCES

INTRODUCTION

1 *Evidence Taken by Her Majesty's Commissioners of Inquiry into the Condition of the Crofters and Cottars in the Highlands and Islands of Scotland* (Edinburgh and London, 1884) [hereafter referred to as 'Napier']: Report, p 127.
2 J. Cameron, *The Old and the New Highlands* (Kirkaldy, 1912), p 25.
3 Dick Scott, *Ask That Mountain: The Story of Parihaka* (Auckland, 1975; 1998).

UNST AND YELL

1 Napier, Question 19721.
2 Wendy Gear, 'Walker: A Wolf in Sheep's Clothing': *New Shetlander* (Lerwick, Voar 1996), p 7.
3 Gear, 'Walker', p 9.
4 Napier, Q.19706.
5 David Craig, *On the Crofters' Trail* (London, 1990), pp 331-2.
6 Personal communication from Mrs Ritch, Gerratoun, Unst.

FETLAR

1 Robert L. Johnson, 'The deserted homesteads of Fetlar': *Shetland Life* (Lerwick, November 1981), p 28.
2 Jane Mack, *Fetlar: The Lairds and Their Estates* (Beach of Houbie, Fetlar, 1993), p 13.
3 Johnson, 'Deserted homesteads', p 33.
4 Johnson, 'Deserted homesteads', p 32.
5 This and much of the following information is based on documents and transcribed oral memoirs filed in the Interpretive Centre, Houbie, Fetlar.
6 Mack, *Fetlar*, p 8.
7 Mack, *Fetlar*, pp 5-6.
8 A. Fenton, *The Northern Isles* (1978; East Linton, 1997), pp 89-91.
9 Johnson, 'Deserted homesteads', p 35.

STRATH NAVER

1 Daniel Defoe, *A Tour Through the Whole Island of Great Britain* (1724- 7; 1962), II, p 416.
2 Napier, QQ.25589-90.
3 John Prebble, *Mutiny* (1975; 1977), pp 140-1.
4 *Papers on the Sutherland Estate Management 1802-1816* (Edinburgh, 1972), I, p 65.

STRATH OF KILDONAN

1 Craig, *On the Crofters' Trail*, plate 3.
2 Donald MacLeod, *Gloomy Memories in the Highlands of Scotland* (Edinburgh, 1841; 3rd ed., Toronto, 1857), p 15.
3 Napier, Q.38219.
4 Napier, Q.38219.
5 Donald Gunn, *History of Manitoba from the Earliest Settlement to 1835* (Ottawa, 1880), pp 89-96, 105, 135, 144.

ASSYNT

1 M. Bangor-Jones, *The Assynt Clearances* (Dundee, 1998), p 51.
2 Bangor-Jones, *Assynt Clearances*, p 31.
3 Bangor-Jones, *Assynt Clearances*, p 31.
4 Bangor-Jones, *Assynt Clearances*, p 36.
5 Napier, Q.27232. MacKenzie had been chosen to speak for Stoer at the commission.
6 Napier, Q.27232.
7 Bangor-Jones, *Assynt Clearances*, p 37.
8 Napier, Q.27639.

COIGACH

1 Eric Richards and Monica Clough, *Cromartie: Highland Life 1650-1914* (Aberdeen, 1989), pp 239-41.
2 Coigach Riots, programme.
3 John R. Baldwin, 'At the Back of the Great Rock: Crofting and Settlement in Coigach, Loch Broom': Baldwin (Ed.), *Peoples and Settlement in Northwest Ross* (Edinburgh, 1994), pp 382-4.
4 Baldwin, 'Great Rock', p 357.
5 Baldwin, 'Great Rock', p 305-6 and fig. 14.12.
6 Baldwin, 'Great Rock', pp 352-5.
7 Richards and Clough, *Cromartie*, p 442.
8 Baldwin, 'Great Rock', p 384.
9 Angus McLeod and Geoff Payne, "Locals" and "Incomers": Social and Cultural Identity in Late Twentieth Century Coigach': Baldwin, *Peoples and Settlement*, p 395.

LECKMELM, BY ULLAPOOL

1 Alexander MacKenzie, *Report on the Leckmelm Evictions, 1882*, quoted in his *The History of the Highland Clearances* (Glasgow, 1883; 1946), pp 159-60.
2 Napier, Q.28630.
3 Napier, Q.28338.
4 Napier, Q.28626.
5 Napier, Q.28551.

STRATH GLASS AND GLEN STRATHFARRAR

1 MacKenzie, *Highland Clearances*, pp 187-90.
2 Napier, Q.41722.
3 Donald Fraser, *Guisachan* (Tomich, 1990; 1998), p 11.
4 Fraser, *Guisachan*, pp 13, 15.
5 Fraser, *Guisachan*, p 31.
6 Information received from George Strachan, Ferry Cottage, Strath Glass.
7 Napier, Q.41722.

KNOYDART

1 Denis Rixson, *Knoydart: A History* (Edinburgh, 1999), pp 134-5.
2 J.M.Bumsted, *The People's Clearance, 1770-1815* (Edinburgh/ Winnipeg, 1982), p xiv.
3 MacKenzie, *Highland Clearances*, pp 174, 179-81.
4 Eric Richards, *The Highland Clearances* (Edinburgh, 2000), p 268.
5 MacKenzie, *Highland Clearances*, pp 173-4.
6 See below, pp 79-83.
7 Rixson, *Knoydart*, maps 7 and 8.
8 John Prebble, *The Highland Clearances* (1963; 1969), pp 278-9.
9 *Minutes of Evidence Taken Before the Royal Commission (Highlands and Islands,1892)* [the 'Deer Forest Commission'] (Edinburgh, 1895), QQ.43229, 43232; Napier, QQ.31836-7.
10 Craig, *On the Crofter's Trail*, p 33; MacLeod, *Gloomy Memories*, pp 137, 167; Prebble, *Highland Clearances*, p 80.

ARISAIG

1 Napier, Q.33127.
2 Napier, Q.32926.
3 Napier, Q.33725.
4 Deer Forest Commission, QQ.50377, 50384.
5 Napier, Q.32767.
6 Deer Forest Commission, Q.50299.
7 Calum Ferguson, *Children of the Black House* (Edinburgh, 2003), p 38.

UNNIMORE, MORVERN

1 Philip Gaskell, *Morvern Transformed* (Cambridge, 1988), p 155.
2 Charles W.J. Withers, *Urban Highlanders, 1700-1900* (East Linton, 1988), pp 86, 147-8.
3 Norman MacLeod, *Reminiscences of a Highland Parish* (1863; n.d.), pp 296-7.
4 MacLeod, *Reminiscences of a Highland Parish*, pp 293-5.

WEST ARDNAMURCHAN

1 *Tuath is Tighearna: Tenants and Landlords*, ed. Donald E. Meek (Edinburgh, 1995), p 192.
2 Photocopy owned by Malcolm MacMillan, Carraig, West Ardnamurchan.
3 Personal communication from Peter MacNab, West Kilbride, Ayrshire. See also his *Highways and Byways in Mull and Iona* (Barr, Ayrshire, 1988), p 27.
4 Napier, Q.36019.
5 Alasdair Maclean, *Night Falls on Ardnamurchan* (1984), pp 40-1.
6 *Oban Times*, April 7 1883.

ULVA

1 Donald W. MacKenzie, *As It Was: Sin Mar a Bha* (Edinburgh, 2000), p 47.
2 Napier, Q.35552.
3 Napier, Q.35552.

COLONSAY

1 Donald A. MacNeill, *Moch is Amnoch*, ed. and trans. Alastair MacNeill Scouler (Colonsay, 1998), p 14.
2 F. Fraser Darling and J. Morton Boyd, *The Highlands and Islands* (1964; 1969), p 42.
3 J. deVere Loder, *Colonsay and Oronsay* (1935; Colonsay, 1995), p 179.
4 Information from *Argyll Colony Plus* (North Caroline Heritage Society), vol.6, no.3. (I owe this reference to Kevin Byrne, Homefield, Colonsay.)
5 Personal communication from Kevin Byrne.
6 MacMillan is a common name both on the Woods Island headstones and on the passenger lists of the ships in 1806: for the lists see Lucille H. Campey, *A Very Fine Class of Immigrants* (Toronto, 2001), pp 116, 118, 124.
7 Personal communication from Kevin Byrne.

RAASAY — HALLAIG AND SCREAPADAL

1 Sorley MacLean, *Reothairt is Contraigh: Spring tide and Neap tide* (Edinburgh, 1977), pp 142-4.
2 Craig, *On the Crofters' Trail*, pp 37-8.
3 Richard Sharpe, *Raasay: a Study in Island History* (1982), p 67.
4 Deer Forest Commission, Q.482; personal communication from John Cummings, Oskaig, Raasay.
5 Deer Forest Commission, Q.361.
6 Deer Forest Commission, Q.510.
7 Sorley MacLean, *Poems 1932-1982* (Philadelphia, 1987), p 174.
8 Fenton, *The Northern Isles*, p 89.
9 Deer Forest Commission, Q.504.

TROTTERNISH, SKYE

1 Maclean, 'An t'Eilean/The Island': *Spring tide and Neap tide*, pp 72-5.
2 Napier, Q.1290.
3 Napier, Q.2143.
4 Napier, Q.1771.
5 Napier, Q.1307.
6 Napier, Q.2825.
7 Napier, QQ.1315, 2804.
8 Napier, Q.1532.
9 Alexander Ross, in *Transactions of the Inverness Scientific and Field Club*, I (December 1877), pp 97-8.

10 Napier, Q.1948.
11 Napier, Q.2364.
12 I.M.M.MacPhail, *The Crofters' War* (Stornoway, 1989), pp 111, 141.
13 MacPhail, *Crofters' War*, pp 129-31.
14 Iain Fraser Grigor, *Mightier Than a Lord* (Stornoway, 1979), pp 114-24 and photograph on p 137.
15 James Hunter, *The Making of the Crofting Community* (Edinburgh, 1976), p 206.

TUASDALE, ISLE OF SKYE

1 Napier, Q.5930.
2 Napier, Q.5932.
3 Napier, Q.5930.
4 John A. Love. *Rum: A Landscape Without Figures* (Edinburgh, 2001), pp 125-9.
5 Napier, Q.6115.
6 Sorley Maclean, *An Cuilithionn/The Cuillin*, II, in *Chapman 52* (Edinburgh 1988), p 47; 'Coilltean Ratharsair/The Woods of Raasay', in *Nua-bhardach Ghaidhlig/Modern Scottish Gaelic Poems*, ed. Donald MacAulay (Edinburgh, 1976), p 102.

BORERAIG, ISLE OF SKYE

1 Maclean, *An Cuilithionn/The Cuillin*, in *Chapman 52*, p 44.
2 Donald Ross, *Real Scottish Grievances* (1854), quoted in MacKenzie, *Highland Clearances*, pp 205-7.
3 Richards, *Highland Clearances*, p 3.
4 Deer Forest Commission, QQ.6931-7006.

STIOMRABHAIGH, LEWIS

1 Napier, QQ.17326, 17675.
2 Angus MacLeod in *Tional*, (Pairc, Lewis) December 1991.
3 Oral memoir by Donald MacDonald, *Lewis: A History of the Island* (Edinburgh, 1978; 1990), p 163; Craig, *On the Crofters' Trail*, p 304.
4 Napier Q.13850.
5 Napier Q.13741.
6 *Diary* for 1851 of John Munro Mackenzie (Stornoway, 1994), pp 33-39.
7 William Mackay in *Report* of the Napier Commissioners, Appendix A, Section XLI (p 160).
8 Adam Nicolson, *Sea Room* (2001), pp 73, 266-7.
9 *Tional*, April 1997.
10 *Tional*, December 1991.

HARRIS, ENSAY, SCALPAY

1 Bill Lawson, *Harris in History and Legend* (Edinburgh, 2002), p 8.
2 Craig, *On the Crofters' Trail*, p 289; Napier, Q.17840.

3 Napier, Q.13205.
4 Napier, Q.18027.

SOLLAS, NORTH UIST.

1 MacKenzie, *Highland Clearances*, pp 198-202.
2 The number evicted is arguable. The *Inverness Courier* for August 1849 gives a figure of 603. The Sheriff-Substitute for the Western Isles disputed this while giving no evidence for a much lower figure (Napier, Q.41434).
3 Napier, Q.41434.
4 Personal communication from Norman Johnston, Lochmaddy.

SOUTH UIST

1 Alexander Carmichael, *Carmina Gadelica* (1900-71; Edinburgh, 1992), pp 36-7 (slightly adapted), 575.
2 Quoted from Ray Burnett, *Benbecula* (Torlum, Benbecula, 1986), p 106.
3 Napier, Q.11675.
4 Angus MacLellan, *The Furrow Behind Me*, trans. John Lorne Campbell (1962), p 7.
5 Napier, Q.13221.
6 Hunter, *Crofting Community*, p 149; Iain Fraser Grigor, *Highland Resistance* (Edinburgh, 2000), pp 96-7; MacLellan, *The Furrow Behind Me*, p 5.
7 Information from the archive of Donald and Jill MacLean in the Cultural Centre, Kildonan, South Uist.
8 *Stories from South Uist* told by Angus MacLellan, trans. John Lorne Campbell (1960; Edinburgh, 1997), p 81.

BARRA

1 MacLeod, *Gloomy Memories*, pp 137-9.
2 Document signed by Beatson and others submitted to Barra Parochial Board: quoted by MacLeod, *Gloomy Memories*, pp 134-5.
3 Alexander Carmichael, *Carmina Gadelica*, III (Edinburgh, 1940), p 111. A painted portrait of Rory Rum is reproduced in Ben Buxton, *Mingulay* (Edinburgh, 1997), plate 21.
4 Donald Buchanan, *Reflections of the Isle of Barra* (1942), pp 45-6.
5 Napier, QQ.10250, 10324-5.

VATERSAY

1 *Report on the Proceedings of the Cottars at Castlebay*, 23 May 1907, quoted from Hunter, *Crofting Community*, pp 189-91.
2 Nan MacKinnon, *Tales, Songs, Tradition from Barra and Vatersay* (Comunn Eachdraidh Bharraidh a. Bhatarsaidh, 1993), pp 30-2.

A' CHAORA MHOR

The Cheviot—a' chaora mhor—whose coming changed the Highlands for ever.